The Olive-Tre
and Other Q

In *The Olive-Tree Bed and Other Quests*, the fourth in the series of Robson Lectures published by the University of Toronto Press, Father Owen Lee studies the quest myth as it occurs in Homer's *Odyssey*, Virgil's *Aeneid*, Wagner's *Parsifal*, and Goethe's *Faust*. Though the four works represent four different genres – oral epic, written epic, music drama, and poetic drama – each deals with the finding of an elusive goal attainable only by the hero called to find it. The questing for the olive-tree bed, the Golden Bough, the Holy Grail, and the Eternal Feminine is, at the deepest level, the hero's search to find the meaning in his life. Though Father Lee's lectures address critical problems in the four works, and draw to some extent on Jungian insights, this volume is also a personal memoir written in the belletristic style for which its author has become known. Father Lee wears his learning lightly, and his writing changes from chapter to chapter as it reflects, in turn, the clarity and naïve sense of wonder in Homer, the darkness and ambivalence in Virgil, the intuitive mysticism of Wagner, and the riotously imaginative exuberance of Goethe. Each of the four quests comes eventually to be seen as every person's search to discover himself – for the journey of the hero is the myth each of us is called to live.

FATHER OWEN LEE, CSB, is a Catholic priest and Professor Emeritus of Classics at St Michael's College, University of Toronto, where he has recently received the Outstanding Teacher Award. Among his many publications are books on Virgil's *Aeneid*, Horace's *Odes*, and Wagner's *Ring*. For many years he has been internationally known as an intermission panellist and commentator on the Metropolitan Opera radio broadcasts.

THE ROBSON CLASSICAL LECTURES

M. OWEN LEE

The Olive-Tree Bed and Other Quests

UNIVERSITY OF TORONTO PRESS
Toronto Buffalo London

ISBN 0-8020-4138-8 (cloth)
ISBN 0-8020-7984-9 (paper)

Printed on acid-free paper

Canadian Cataloguing in Publication Data

Lee, M. Owen, 1930–
   The olive-tree bed and other quests

   (The Robson classical lectures)
   Includes bibliographical references and index.
   ISBN 0-8020-4138-8 (bound)   ISBN 0-8020-7984-9 (pbk.)

   1. Quests in literature.   2. Heroes in literature.
   I. Title.   II. Series

   PN56.Q47L43 1996   809'.93351   C96-932151-1

Portions of chapter 3 are reprinted from *Fathers and Sons in Virgil's Aeneid* by M. Owen Lee. By permission of the State University of New York Press. © 1979

Portions of chapter 4 are reprinted from *First Intermissions* by M. Owen Lee. By permission of Oxford University Press, Inc. © 1995

University of Toronto Press acknowledges the financial assistance to its publishing program of the Canada Council and the Ontario Arts Council.

For
IRENE SLOAN
GEORGE MARTIN
and all who guided my steps

Contents

Foreword

This is the fourth volume of the Robson Classical Lectures to reach publication. The series takes its name from Donald Oakley Robson (1905–76), who graduated in Honours Classics from Victoria College in the University of Toronto in 1928. He went on to earn his MA (1929) and his PhD (1932) from the University of Toronto. After teaching at the University of Western Ontario for seventeen years, he returned to his *alma mater*, and taught Latin there from 1947 until his retirement in 1975. His wife, Rhena Victoria Kendrick (1901–82), also graduated in Honours Classics from Victoria College, in 1923, with the Governor General's Gold Medal. They were generous benefactors of their college. In Professor Robson's will he made provision that, from time to time, several public lectures should be delivered on a classical theme by a distinguished scholar, and then, after appropriate revision, published.

The series as a whole will, we believe, have a wide appeal among those who are interested in ancient Greece and Rome, and in the culture of classical antiquity. We were fortunate to persuade Father Owen Lee, Professor of Classics at the University of Toronto, to participate in our project. As an undergraduate he was a student of Professor Robson, and graduated from St Michael's College in 1953. After earning his doctorate from the University of British Columbia, he returned to Toronto in 1960, and taught here for the next thirty-five years, with brief interludes at Houston (1968–72) and Chicago (1972–5). He is perhaps best known for his regular appearances on the broadcasts of the

Metropolitan Opera. In October 1995 he presented three lectures on 'The Quest' at Victoria College. They were greatly appreciated by his audience, which included both specialists and non-specialists; it was clear that they would provide the basis for a sound, scholarly, innovative book. We now present that book, a distinguished contribution to a distinguished series.

Wallace McLeod
for the Committee, 1996

MEMBERS OF THE COMMITTEE (1992–6)
J.M. Bigwood
J.N. Grant, *ex officio*
A.M. Keith
W.E. McLeod
K.R. Thompson
J.S. Traill, *Chairman*
E.I. Robbins, *ex officio*

Preface

Donald Oakley Robson taught me Virgil at Victoria College when I was a student in Honour Classics at the University of Toronto. The year was 1951–2. The course was a classic journey through thousands of hexameter verses. The discoveries were legion.

Some forty years later I was invited by Wallace E. McLeod, who was with me as a student in that Virgil class, to give three public lectures in memory of that beloved teacher, at the college that was his for many years, in the very building in which he taught, and on the subject in which he had instructed me. It was an invitation I could not, on the occasion of my own retirement from the teaching of Classics, even think of refusing.

The book that has resulted represents, not the largely philological scholarship favoured at the time of my undergraduate instruction, and not the paraliterary critical methods in vogue today, but a genre esteemed then and fast disappearing now, a genre once affectionately called belles-lettres: I have in chapters 2, 3, and 4, which are the substance of the three Robson lectures, concerned myself almost exclusively with what I have found beautiful in the *Odyssey*, in the *Aeneid* and, as a treatment of opera was expected of me, in Wagner's *Parsifal*. If I have addressed some critical problems in those works, and provided endnotes thereto (not a practice usually associated with belles-lettres), the problems are at least perennial concerns that today's readers will, I hope, still find interesting. In the lectures, which were intended for 'a general university audience,' I found it necessary for my purposes to include a fair amount of plot summary – especially on *Parsifal*, which would be less familiar to classicists than the other works – and I have kept much of that summary here in the published chapters. I have also availed myself of the Jungian insights that helped me in writing my three books on Virgil. Finally, I felt entitled by the occasion to cast a paragraph or two in each chapter in the form of a personal memoir.

For publication I was invited by the Robson Classical Lectures committee to add a fourth work to the three I dealt with orally. In discussing Goethe's *Faust* I allowed the belletristic approach, the plot summary, and the half-century-old memories of student days to run imaginatively riot. That seemed one way of dealing with a sometimes riotously imaginative work that for this non-specialist in German occupies something of a mid-place between the hexameter epics of Homer and Virgil and the last music drama of Richard Wagner. Finally, in brief introductory and concluding chapters I have drawn somewhat obliquely on two other works, *Don Quixote* and *The Epic of Gilgamesh*, that deal with my theme, which is the hero's quest.

I should like to thank Professors Wallace E. McLeod, Emmet I. Robbins, and John S. Traill of the Robson Classical Lectures committee for choosing me to give the talks, and Suzanne Rancourt and John St James of the University of Toronto Press for seeing them past the editing stages and into print. I should also like to thank the three anonymous readers who commented on the manuscript, James K. Farge, who helped with the proof-reading, and Oxford University Press and State University of New York Press for permission to use, in considerably expanded form, material first published in my books *First Intermissions* and *Fathers and Sons in Virgil's Aeneid*.

St Michael's College,
University of Toronto

THE OLIVE-TREE BED AND OTHER QUESTS

CHAPTER ONE

Questing

At the beginning of the questing book to end all questing books, the author says, not without rue, 'Idling reader, you may believe me when I tell you that I should have liked this book, which is the child of my brain, to be the fairest, the sprightliest, and the cleverest that could be imagined; but I have not been able to contravene the law of nature which would have it that like begets like.'

I should have liked to have written that sentence, for it says what must be said at the start of this book. (Fortunately, scholarly convention allows me to quote it.[1]) This book on what is perhaps the vastest of all myths is only as fair, sprightly, and clever as its author was permitted by nature to be.

I shall not tell here of the quests of Don Quixote, which the above quotation first introduced, but my pages will surely strike many as quixotic. They treat four of the great questing works of art by way of personal reflection. They are light and leitmotivic. They do not, and are not intended to, advance the cause of scholarship. My best hope is that in these chapters I might encourage you, idling reader, to renew your acquaintance with, or perhaps become acquainted for the first time with, and learn to wonder more about, the four questing works we shall consider together.

The works are either epics or works that have grown somewhat quixotically out of the epic tradition. Epic defines a man not as *homo sapiens* or as *homo ludens* but as *homo viator* – man on a journey.[2] I shall attempt to define that journey as it appears in the first and best of all masters of epic, Homer, and thereafter to add to the definition details from Virgil, Wagner, and Goethe. But first we must make some preliminary remarks.

The quests we shall discuss have a number of features in common. Our two classical heroes may travel over seas and our two Romantics across landscapes, but all four have amorous encounters, fight decisive battles, and face more-than-mortal dangers en route, and if only three of them actually visit the Underworld ('that deep, dark place in the self where the roots of the self begin'[3]), the fourth, Parsifal, may be thought to have done so symbolically. All four, accordingly, require more than their own resources to reach their goals. Only one, Aeneas, has a divinity for a parent, but all of them depend on supernatural assistance, be it from gods or God or a near-divine Eternal Feminine, for the achieving of their goals. The four works are also linked, though this is only a fortuitous connection, by arboreal imagery: Odysseus finds the object of his quest in a bed he has rounded from the trunk of an olive tree; Aeneas finds his Golden Bough on an oak in a dense forest; Parsifal finds his Holy Grail in a forest-encircled castle; Faust resumes his quest, after his creator had laid it aside for many years, in a shaded Alpine glen alive with voices. Accordingly, I agreed to give the lectures on which this book is based on condition that I could speak them in front of the five great curving picture windows at Victoria College, against a backdrop of waving trees in full October colours.

There are other features common to the four quests. Each of the heroes is tempted to tarry, in effect to abandon his journey, and must resist that temptation. (With Faust this becomes the very essence of the questing.) All four heroes, being human after all, may be thought to have failed to some degree. I shall not attempt at any length to explain the savagery of Odysseus's first adventure after leaving Troy, of Aeneas's blood-lust on the field of battle, of Parsifal's almost murderous reaction when Kundry calls him a fool, and of Faust's callous betrayal of Gretchen or of his wish, brought to fulfilment, that those who will not conform to his view of progress be destroyed. I shall only say that these are faults, writ large, that can be found in smaller measure in any of us who are human. The quest requires that the quester face up to all that lies within himself

– the destructive as well as the creative impulses, the hurt and the hate as well as the longing and the promise. Small wonder that the quester sometimes fails.

The character of each hero varies from culture to culture: Odysseus is *polytropos*, Aeneas a man of *pietas*, Parsifal a knight learning chivalry and compassion, Faust an ardently self-absorbed intellectual. Characteristics of the Greek, the Roman, the medieval, and the enlightened German Romantic are grafted on to the mythic figure of the quester. But the questing hero is recognizable in them all. And despite the generic differences in the four works – oral epic, written epic, music drama, poetic drama – the notion of the quest remains in them essentially unchanged. The objective for our heroes is not so much the righting of wrongs in the world (the avowed purpose of the Arthurian knight) as the finding of an elusive goal attainable only by the one man chosen to find it (the declared purpose of the mythic hero). The questing of each of our four figures is, at the deepest level, the hero's search to find the meaning of his life.

We are not, then, surprised to discover that the typical questing hero is no youth but a man in middle age, in the second half of his life when, disenchanted with his earlier successes and conscious too of his failures, he grows increasingly aware of his mortality. He is ready at last to listen to his inner voices, to reconcile inner conflicts, to search for a deeper meaning in the adventures he has passed through. Parsifal alone of our four heroes is young, and even he is a mature man when his quest is completed: his wanderings, his despairing, and his aging are depicted in the musical prelude to the last act of his opera.

And even as the four heroes we shall consider are mature men, so the four works mark the second half, indeed the final years, of the lives of their respective creators. The *Odyssey* was described by Longinus (9.13) as a work of Homer's maturity, 'like the sun at its setting – the intensity is gone, but the grandeur remains.' The ten years Virgil spent on the *Aeneid* were his last years. So were the five years the aging Wagner spent on *Parsifal*, though the work was germinating in his mind for more than thirty years before he began it. The two parts of Goethe's *Faust* mark his youth and, some sixty years later, his old age. The questing works are the works of men at the end of the journeys that were their lives.

The hero's quest has, almost as a matter of course, attracted the attention of psychologists and psychiatrists, who have contended that in the quest myth the psyche, in the figure of the hero, acknowledges its incompleteness: it searches for something in the dark of a forest or on the edge of the world – that is to say, in its own depths or at the limits of conscious experience – that will explain it to itself. The different phases of the journey may then represent the development and transformations of the psyche in its journey through life, and indeed each of our journeying heroes seems to encounter what since Jung, and to some extent before Jung, we have called the archetypes – the memories, stirrings, fears, and longings that we all have felt and which have manifested themselves in images that recur in the folklore of the world[4] and in virtually all mythologies.

Our four myths are male myths, though of course women are very important in them (and female psychology has its corresponding archetypes and its own myths, legends, and folklore). The male hero in myth experiences what, according to Nietzsche and to some thinkers before and many after Nietzsche,[5] every man experiences every night in dreams, as his psychic system adjusts itself to his conscious life.

I certainly feel that the extraordinary power exerted by the four works we shall consider is due in some part to our recognizing in them, however unconsciously, those archetypal encounters. Homer, Virgil, Wagner, and Goethe all draw on mythic material that is centuries older than themselves, and to a considerable extent the greatness of their works is the result of their having realized the potential of the human experience that lies half-remembered in the myths they use.

The fundamental archetype for our purposes is that of the journey itself, the hero's searching for something that can explain his existence and transform it. If this is most often seen as an inner journey, it has its outer dimension as well. Even as science has come to see the structure of the smallest atom as identical to that of the whole solar system, so myth speaks of a correspondence between the contents of the individual human pysche and the observable laws of the cosmos: what happens within us also happens in the world beyond us. The voyage of the hero is like the voyage of the sun. The sun, in mythic thought, journeys daily around the earth, continuing its night journey under the earth to be reborn the next morning – and some kind of rebirth inevitably marks the meridian of the hero's journey. Of our four heroes, Odysseus, who has been thought originally to have been a solar deity, ends his journeying deposited on the shore of his Ithaca blanketed and sleeping, awaiting the dawn, like a newborn infant. Aeneas, who is compared in similes to the sun god Apollo, must before he begins his battles be instructed by his father, in a sunlit field beneath the earth, in the mysteries of rebirth and reincarnation. Parsifal's journey reaches its climax on a bright morning when all of nature is reborn. And Faust, who at the mid-point of his journeying renews himself by contemplating the reflection of the sun in nature's wonders, is reborn in Goethe's final pages as after his death his soul mounts skywards as the 'spirit-peer' of newborn children.

In our century the mythic journey of the hero has been mapped with new precision by Carl Jung. How successful the pattern has been in the clinical uses of psychology I leave to others to say. There is little question that it helps explain much that has hitherto been unexplained in intuitive works of art that are fashioned from myth.[6] For Jung and his followers, the journeying hero encounters four main archetypes – the shadow, the anima, the Wise Old Man, and the self. These we may briefly detail.

The Jungian shadow is a figure of the same sex as the hero, but in all ways opposite to the sunlit hero's own persona. The shadow is not, as is sometimes thought, evil; he is an embodiment of what the hero has repressed or denied in himself. The shadow can be sinister, capable even of bringing the hero to ruin, but this will only happen if he, the shadow, remains unacknowledged. The successful hero befriends his shadow, as Faust takes Mephistopheles for his companion, for the shadow contributes aspects of humanity – often animalistic, primitive, and instinctual – that are not a part of the hero's conscious persona. This first figure the hero encounters on his way to the discovery of the self is already a 'part-self,'[7] a completion. It also points the way to the next archetype, the anima.

The anima is the feminine element in a man, often shaped by his experience of his own mother. The hero's anima can, when encountered, clear the way for him to reach profound inner depths. But at first it can, like the shadow, prove malevolent, and it has even more destructive power than the shadow has. It is characteristic of the anima, when it cannot utterly destroy the hero, to attempt by any means it can to arrest his onward journey. And yet the anima, potentially destructive, proves, when its destructive aspect is defeated, to be creative, positive, healing, and helpful. The seductive but ultimately helpful women Odysseus encounters on his journeys, the goddess mother who arrests Aeneas's voyage but then sends her doves to direct him to his father, the Kundry who is so ambivalent in *Parsifal*, and the Eternal Feminine that, we discover in the last line of *Faust*, has always led the hero onwards – these are the mythic aspects of woman encountered by questing man. Joseph Campbell, charting his way through many mythologies, has described this archetype in a well-known paragraph:

Woman, in the picture language of mythology, represents the totality of what can be known. The hero is the one who comes to know. As he progresses in the slow initiation which is life, the form of the goddess undergoes for him a series of transfigurations: she can never be greater than himself, though she can always promise more than he is yet capable of comprehending. She lures, she guides, she bids him burst his fetters. And if he can match her import, the two, the knower and the known, will be released from every limitation. Woman is the guide to the sublime acme of sensuous adventure. By deficient eyes she is reduced to inferior states; by the evil eye of ignorance she is spellbound to banality and ugliness. But she is redeemed by the eyes of understanding. The hero who can take her as she is, without undue commotion but with the kindness and assurance she requires, is potentially the king, the incarnate god, of her created world.[8]

When a hero has successfully defeated the dangerous potential and assimilated the benevolent and creative aspects of his inner feminine, he encounters, usually with the aid of the anima, something of still greater benefit to himself in Jung's next archetype, the Wise Old Man. While the first two archetypes actively confront the hero, the Wise Old Man must be sought out. He is difficult to find, often evasive, and his advice may seem less helpful to the hero than that offered by the tamed anima, because it is advice that leads the hero, not to the solution of immediate problems, but to his final discovery of himself. The Wise Old Man, who is in many myths the hero's father (in the Parsifal tradition, and in a number of other medieval tales, he is the hero's maternal uncle). So the mythic journey often becomes the hero's search to have the mother's promise ratified by the father. Symbolically, the hero must *become* his mother and his father in order to become himself.

If the hero is destined to complete his quest he finds, finally, a sign that he has reached the centre of all that he has experienced and learned. He finds, in more psychological terms, a sign that the opposing forces within him have been reconciled. A sign of the self. The terminology is, once again, Jung's, who finds this goal of a man's search for wholeness expressed in such circular designs as the sun, the rose window of a cathedral, the ring of bright water, or, to cite Jung's favourite design, the Tibetan and Indian mandala (a Sanskrit word for circle), which for therapeutic purposes he encouraged his patients to create for themselves. As Joseph Campbell put it shortly before his death, the mandala is

a circle that is coordinated or symbolically designed so that it has the meaning of a cosmic order. When composing mandalas, you are trying to coordinate your personal circle with the universal circle. In a very elaborate Buddhist mandala, for example, you have the deity in the center as the power source, the illumination source. The peripheral images would be manifestations or aspects of the deity's radiance ... Making a mandala is a discipline for pulling [the] scattered aspects of your life together, for finding a center and ordering yourself to it.[9]

One such circular image appears in a fourteenth-century manuscript of the epic *Lancelot du Lac*:[10] the Holy Grail is placed by two angels in the midst of the knights assembled around the Round Table. T.S. Eliot may have sensed this notion of the discovery of the self at the centre of experience, of rest at the centre of unrest, when in *Four Quartets* he spoke of 'the still point of the turning world' (*Burnt Norton* 62).

The mythic hero thus faces the archetypes within him, clarifies them (Jung's 'individuation process'), learns from them, and eventually effects a synthesis of them (the 'Viveka' of Hindu and Buddhist thought). The grave mistakes the hero makes are essential to his questing, for our errors, as Freud has taught us, result from conflicts that must be resolved. Knight-errant means not only wandering knight but erring knight. A hero must stray from the true path of his questing if he is eventually to succeed in finding his goal.

All of this might be supplemented with details provided, rather famously, by Lord Raglan and Joseph Campbell in their composite heroes – the former with his twenty-two points, the latter with his monomyth of the hero and his initiatory rites of passage. But I should like instead to trace the archetypal pattern in the earliest questing myth left to us – that found in the Sumerian *Epic of Gilgamesh*. Most of what is common to the four quests we shall consider was vividly prefigured in this poem that antedates Homer by more than a thousand years and, like Homer, seems to be the result of a centuries-long process of adaptation of older materials. I shall tell the Gilgamesh story in four paragraphs, each of them centred around one of the four archetypes.

Gilgamesh, king of Uruk and son of the goddess Ninsun, being two parts god and one part man, surpasses all his people in courage, beauty, and strength. But he cannot in his human nature satisfy his immortal longings, and his exhausted people ask the gods to give him a companion who will be his complement. The gods fashion Enkidu, a creature more bestial than human till he is tamed and to some degree civilized by a wise but lowly woman. When the godlike Gilgamesh encounters the animalistic Enkidu, he wrestles with him, throws him, and takes him for his companion. To win the fame decreed for him by his destiny, Gilgamesh journeys with Enkidu through a forest and up a mountain, where he fells the great cedar tree guarded by the evil giant Humbaba. Prompted by his companion, he cuts off the monster's head.

The goddess of love, Ishtar, is thereupon filled with desire for Gilgamesh. But he, knowing how dangerous she has proved to all her previous lovers, rejects her. Furious, she asks the father god to send the Bull of Heaven to destroy Gilgamesh, who with the aid of Enkidu slays the bull. The gods then punish him by causing his companion to fall sick and die, and Gilgamesh in his grief feels compassion for the first time. He also decides that death shall never claim him as it has his friend.

Though the sun god predicts that he will never achieve complete immortality, Gilgamesh traces the journey of the sun beneath the earth till he reaches the Waters of Death, which he is able to cross when the woman Siduri (who may be a form of Ishtar) helpfully directs him to Urshanabi, the ferryman of the dead. Beyond the Waters of Death Gilgamesh meets his own forefather, the old and now immortal Utnapishtim, who narrates the epic's famous story of the flood, and tells the hero that he can achieve immortality only if he finds and plucks a mysterious underwater plant whose thorns will prick his hand.

Gilgamesh finds the plant and plucks it, but then sights a well of cool water, bathes in it, and loses the plant to the well's serpent – which promptly sloughs its skin, reborn. The epic ends where it began, with Gilgamesh, mortal after all but assured that immortality is not his destiny, returned a wiser man to his kingdom and his subjects.

The heroic quest seems always to end where it began, though, as Northrop Frye has observed, 'the starting point [has been] renewed and transformed by the quest itself.'[11] So it is that Homer arranges his many Odyssean stories so that we who listen hear first of an Ithaca disrupted and finally, after the hero's journey there and eventual victory over his enemies, of an Ithaca at peace. So it is that Virgil's hero leads his people from a fallen Troy on a long journey (the very name Troy seems to mean labyrinthine wandering[12]) to an Italy that, we eventually discover, was the Trojans' ancestral home. So it is that Wagner shapes a bewildering mass of Grail legends into a beautifully proportioned structure in which Act III of his *Parsifal* is a recapitulation of Act I, with the discord resolved and the Grail restored to wholeness. And so it is that Goethe begins his *Faust* with a scene in which archangels look down from heaven to a turbulent earth and ends it with a spiraling ascent from a troubled earth to a rapturous heaven. In each case the end is the beginning, because what is sought for and found on the journey is in some way within the hero from the start. The quest was learning how to see.

T.S. Eliot writes, at the end of *Four Quartets*:

> We shall not cease from exploration
> And the end of all our exploring
> Will be to arrive where we started
> And know the place for the first time.
>   (*Little Gidding* 239–42)

Here Eliot says what *Gilgamesh* said more than four thousand years earlier: at the end of his journey a man comes at last to know what, all along, he has been and is.

Myth, it has been said, is something that never was but always is. A millennium and a half earlier than even the earliest of our four works, we find, in an epic lost for thousands of years and surviving in an incomplete form, the hero in search of an elusive destiny, the companion shadow, the encounters with a feminine at first malevolent and then helpful, the revelation provided by a wise old man, and the hero's discovery, in a context of rebirth, of the self that has always been his.

This is the principal mythic pattern I shall avail myself of in speaking of the *Odyssey*, the *Aeneid*, *Parsifal*, and *Faust*. I do not offer it as any kind of solution to the many critical problems to be found in the four works, or as a demonstration of what accounts for their greatness. The same pattern, after all, may be traced in any number of works of lesser stature. But I do feel that the archetype of the quest underlies and to some extent shapes each work – providing Homer with the means whereby he can give point to what before him were probably isolated sea stories, supplying Virgil with a metaphoric mirror to reflect the *res gestae* of one of the great figures of history, enabling Wagner to compress a mass of mythic and philosophic material into a vast symmetrical structure, and allowing Goethe eventually to save the man who for centuries had been the very symbol of damnation.

It is not my purpose to force any of the four works I shall speak of into some archetypal mould, let alone (*absit!*) to presume to censure any of the four artists for failure to understand his myth when the finished poem or drama does not correspond in every detail to the patterns Jung and others have traced. But I do hope to show that each of the four artists has sensed something of the same questing myth and interpreted it according to his own understanding. This is not to equate any of the works with the myth that underlies all four. Great works of art are much more than the archetypes that underlie them.

As I have bid the classroom farewell, and may rightly regard this as the last effort of my academic pen, I'd like to end this beginning by borrowing, with slight adaptations, another quotation from the creator of that questing *hidalgo* from La Mancha, and once again from the author's opening page:

How can you expect me not to be concerned over what that venerable legislator, the Public, will say when it sees me, at my age, presenting for publication a book that is a stranger to invention, paltry in style, impoverished in content, and wholly lacking in learning and wisdom, without marginal citations or notes at the end of the book when other works of this sort, even though they be fabulous and profane, are so packed with maxims from Aristotle and Plato and the whole crowd of philosophers as to fill the reader with admiration and lead him to regard the author as a well read, learned, and eloquent individual? Not to speak of the citations from Holy Writ! All of this my book will lack, for I have no citations for the margins, no notes for the end ...

Señor Cervantes made those remarks to a clever friend who found him with his pen lodged idly over his ear, his elbow on the table, and his chin in his hand. The friend laughed out loud at the author's naiveté and promptly instructed him in the uses of scholarly aids. I have listened a little to that clever friend – a

member, in fact, of the Robson Classical Lecture committee –
and my book comes to you adorned with some academic appara-
tus. But you will not be fooled. This is a not a book to set beside
those of the men who have preceded me in the series known now
as the distinguished Robson Lectures. It is a book compounded of
memories and imaginings, of classroom chalk dust and of the
enthusiasms, the reflections, and the dreams of a man who, if he
could have, would have been a hero, but had to settle for the kind
of questing all men do in the course of an ordinary life.

CHAPTER TWO

The Olive-Tree Bed

'Hush,' says the father to his son as they both near the completion of their quests. 'The Olympians have ways of their own. Off to bed now.'

Homer's *Odyssey* is, among many other things, the best of all bedside books. A significant part of it, Books 9 to 12, comprises tales you likely first heard in childhood, perhaps as your mother or father put you to sleep. And Books 13 to 24, the last half of the *Odyssey*, tell a tale in which revelations seem to pass freely from one pillow to another. Homer's poem is about a very wide-awake and active man, an alert thinker, an accomplished liar who proudly says of himself, 'The whole world knows my stratagems.' But it is also true that sleep saves this wide-awake Odysseus more than once from disaster, and that warnings and intimations come to him, and to his wife Penelope, in semi-conscious states. Some revelations, Penelope tells us, come not through the ivory gate of empty dreams but through the gate of horn whereby true dreams find fulfilment. She should know, for she is one of literature's great intuitors.[1]

So if, gentle reader, you're inclined while reading this chapter to nod off, as I often am at my age over a good story, so much the better, provided that when you nod off you dream a little.

The hero of the *Odyssey* acknowledges and values the revelations that come from sleep, dreams, and divine visitations – from what we may call the intuitive part of his nature. He knows that it isn't just physical strength that is needed to string a hero's bow and shoot an arrow straight. It is many things besides: mental concentration, good breeding, the skill that comes only from practice, and above all the divine aid that only a hero can call upon. When, at the climax of his epic, Odysseus proves the string on his great bow, Homer tells us that it gives off the sound of a swallow's note. Surely, we think, Homer introduces a swallow at that moment because the hero has come home, as the swallow does in season.[2] But there is, I suspect, something more to it than that. This swallow's note is followed by a thunderclap from Zeus. And soon Zeus's daughter Athene appears, to preside over the hero's triumph in the form of a swallow, darting up to the smoky rafters of Odysseus's house as he slays the dastardly suitors. At that moment, a power beyond his own is with Odysseus, as he himself would be the first to admit.

All four of the questing figures we shall consider in these chapters are in touch with sources of more than physical, more than human, strength. They respect those sources, commune with them, and pray to them. (Even that Enlightenment hero, Goethe's Faust, prays to nature.) And Homer's *Odyssey* tells us on page after page that we come in contact with those sources of strength most often in sleep and dreams.

So do, if you care to, nod off. Homer himself, we are told, sometimes nodded.

Having said that in deference to dreams, the intuitive, and the more-than-mortal, I'll begin with an attempt at a rational definition. What is a quest? We'll develop a kind of answer here over several chapters, but a partial description comes in the opening lines of our first poem: *Andra moi, ennepe, Mousa, polytropon ...*

Sing to me, O Muse, of that resourceful man who roamed the wide world after he had sacked the holy city of Troy, who saw the cities of many people and learned their ways, who suffered to his heart's depth many hardships on the sea, seeking to save his life and bring his comrades home, and even so did not save them, though he wanted sore to do so. (1.1–6)

That – wandering, seeing, learning, suffering and, yes, to some extent failing – describes the quest in our four works. In the *Odyssey*, the happiest of the quests, the 'resourceful man' eventually rises above his failures, triumphs over his opponents, and finds at last what he has been searching for. But Homer doesn't mention all of those things – 'to strive, to seek, to find, and not to yield' – in his prologue. He saves much of the striving and all of the finding for the rest of the poem, into which, after the prologue, he immediately plunges.

In medias res. As we begin the poem, it is nine years since the fall of Troy, and nineteen since Odysseus first left for Troy. The moment of *kairos* has come with the twentieth year. Everything is ready for the completion of the hero's quest, his arrival home. The sea god Poseidon, who has prevented that fulfilment, has gone off to visit the innocent Ethiops who live on the edges of the world. The other gods meet in council. Zeus complains – and it is a consideration largely new with the *Odyssey* – that humankind blame the gods for their troubles, when actually it is their own wickedness that brings sorrows upon them.

Now a part of the long quest tradition is that the quester be innocent, or at least cleansed of guilt, when he reaches his goal. The wily Odysseus is not innocent in the sense in which the Ethiops, with whom the gods periodically dine, or in the sense in which the Grail knights, who have the strength of ten because their hearts are pure, are innocent. But in what has Odysseus offended? Are we to think of him and the other Greeks who sacked what Homer often calls 'the holy city of Troy' as guilty? No – in Homer, the Greeks feel sorrow for the suffering they inflicted at Troy, but not guilt. Is Odysseus's offence, then, having lost all of his Ithacans on the return trip? No – Homer makes it clear that, save for the few unfortunates lost to the monsters Polyphemus and Scylla, the crew have brought their fates upon themselves despite Odysseus's warnings. Is Odysseus being punished, then, for blinding (in what may rightly be thought self-defence) the cyclops Polyphemus, who is Poseidon's son? That has offended Poseidon, surely, but the other gods seem not to regard it as an act involving guilt. Is he being punished, then, for his incorrigible and inveterate fibbing? No, for such deceptions are required for survival in an Odyssean world fraught with dangers. Has Odysseus offended the gods for having spent long nights of love on the way home with Calypso and Circe? Hardly. Not even Penelope reproaches him for that.

No, over the years of wandering Odysseus has suffered, not for any failures,[3] but – here, as often in Homer, we see the beginnings of the tragic ethos – so that he might learn. *Pathei mathos.* He has had, first, to unlearn through suffering the Bronze Age ethic that made him a good fighter at Troy. The gods punish him when his first post-war exploit is to sack another city, slay its men, and distribute its women and substance among his own followers. Zeus sends a terrible storm to blow Odysseus off course as he rounds the Peloponnese and makes for Ithaca. The hero has to learn, through four books of further adventures, the new Odyssean virtues that will equip him to return home a proper father, husband, and king.[4] Fortunately for him, it is his nature to learn. And the gods in the *Odyssey*, we discover before we have turned the first page of the poem, are interested in helping mortals to learn.

In Book 1 the gods put their heads together to find a way to get the hero home. There are two plans: Hermes will this very day command the nymph Calypso to release Odysseus from her island, Ogygia, while Athene will speed off to the island of Ithaca to send Odysseus's nineteen-year-old son, Telemachus, in search of his missing father.

So there might be said to be two quests in the poem – the larger adventures of the mature, homeward-faring hero, and the 'little quest' of his young son in search of him. I'd like to spend some of my time here on that 'little quest,' the *Telemacheia*, the first four books of the *Odyssey*, because another thing we can say about questing is that a hero's search – for the Golden Bough, the Holy Grail, or some other symbolic object – is at least partly the search for his father. 'It's a wise child,' says young Telemachus as he is being readied for his quest in Book 1, 'who knows his own father.'

'These things lie on the lap of the gods,' Athene tells the boy, challenging him to cooperate with her divine aid even as his father has. 'You are no longer a child. Off with you to Pylos to consult with godlike Nestor about your father. And then to Sparta, to fair-haired Menelaus.' Those father-figures will know, if anyone knows, where the father the boy has never known might still be found.

'Sir,' says Telemachus (for Athene is disguised as a father-figure, Mentes), 'You have spoken to me like a father to his son' (1.216, 267, 284–308).

My first invitation to travel came in 1963 when, after several discouraging setbacks, the moment of *kairos* finally came: I was awarded a scholarship for study at the American School of Classical Studies in Athens. I suppose that Professor Gertrude Smith was my Athene. She was the one who announced to me at last that the necessary funding was available, and wished me godspeed. Like Telemachus, I promptly paid a visit to two households to seek information.

I visited first, not sandy Pylos, but Drive Ridge Park, where my hosts were carving meat in lavish portions. Professor Donald Oakley Robson told me, Nestorlike but not at Nestorian length, that the Europe I would see would be, first and foremost, not a collection of art galleries, opera houses, and cathedrals, but the cities of many people of many different languages and cultures, all of them strenuously occupied in the business of daily living, and that I had best occupy myself with studying their ways and learning from them. Then Mrs Robson, knowing that Greece was my ultimate destination, and sensing that I needed some goal for my questing, recalled her first visit to Olympia, and the first sight of the monument that was for her the grail to be sought for in Greece – the Nike of Paeonius. Finding the way to it was not an easy quest for her, as I recall. But when she arrived wearied before the statue of the luminous goddess, she told me, she stayed in wonder before it till its peace had filled her soul.

Secondly, this inexperienced Telemachus visited, if not quite the gold-gleaming palace of Menelaus and Helen, the hospitable household of that then-young classicist most knowledgeable in the uses of the ancient bow, Wallace McLeod. He told me of the wonders he had seen and the cities he had visited in the Aegean, and tested my rudimentary knowledge of modern Greek. Then the lovely Mrs McLeod, like Helen with her basket and ball of yarn, settled down with us after dinner and, sensing what I needed most – a goal for my striving – said she remembered best, of her travels in Greece, the temple of another luminous goddess. The Parthenon, the temple of Athene, was to her *quod unum est pro laboribus tantis*.

Therein lies a new detail in our definition of the quest: the male's questing for his father and his self means, in the *Odyssey* and elsewhere, paying special attention to the women he meets, for, Homer tells us, wonderful as men are, women are the more perceptive of the species. When young Telemachus arrives at Sparta, Menelaus doesn't know who he is. But Helen says, instantly, 'Never have I seen such a likeness! Surely this is Odysseus's son.' Only then does Menelaus say, 'Now that you point out the resemblance, I see it too' (4.140–8). In that exchange, Helen and Menelaus state an Odyssean motif: women are more perceptive than men, and men must graciously concur in this.[5] Odysseus himself must, at the end of the poem, concur in this. Jasper Griffin notes in addition that when Telemachus leaves the palace at Sparta, Menelaus gives him 'a foolish present which has to be changed,' while Helen gives him 'a suggestive one, a wedding dress for his bride.'[6] The perceptive Helen knows what the completion of an Odyssean quest involves.

Every commentator on the *Odyssey* notes the special importance of the women in it. But the beginning of a mythic hero's quest means – a further detail in our definition – severing the bond with women until the young man is ready to relate maturely to them. Telemachus must leave his mother to find his father. Because he has been nineteen years growing up without his father, he is powerless to prevent the exploitation of his mother by the suitors who have come one-hundred-strong to ask for her hand and have crassly taken possession of her palace. Telemachus takes leave of his mother without a farewell. 'I don't want tears to spoil her lovely cheeks,' he tells his old nurse, Eurycleia, in his new determination to leave home.

Women in Homer know that questing means leaving them in search of illumination. Telemachus must seek what lies beyond his insular world. Eurycleia sees this, as Homer tells us in an accumulation of charming and lightly symbolic details:

Telemachus went off to bed, up where his room was built high in the fair court, in a place that let him look off far and wide. He was pondering many things in his heart. Eurycleia lit his way with blazing torches ... She of all the serving women loved him most, and she had nursed him when he was a little child. He opened the doors of his fair-wrought chamber, and sat on his bed and took off his soft doublet. This he laid in the hands of the wise old woman, and she folded it and smoothed it out and hung it on a peg by the ornamental bedstead. Then she took leave of the chamber and closed the door by its silver handle, and slid the bolt across by its thong. There all night long, wrapped in his fleece of sheep's wool, Telemachus pondered in his heart the journey that Athene had put there. (1.425–44)

The passage, replete with the externalized description that Erich Auerbach admired in Homer, implies more than it says on the surface: woman knows what the prospective hero must do by way of preparation for his quest; she lights him and leads him to the bedroom that looks out in all directions, to the bed where illumination comes in sleep – and she ceremoniously leaves him there to search his inward heart, where a luminous goddess has planted divine yearnings. If the hero's search is the search for his father and his masculine self, it is an Eternal Feminine – as Goethe was to remind us centuries after Homer – that leads him onwards.

The sense of ceremony as Telemachus is put to bed is also very Odyssean. Questing in Homer's poem would be impossible without – next detail – the ceremonious hospitality that, in respect for Zeus Xenios, Homeric civilization traditionally extends. The reason why the suitors' offence is so great, and is given so terrible a punishment when Odysseus finally arrives among them, is that they have offended against *xenia*, hospitality. The world of the *Odyssey* is a world in which survival depends on each community offering ceremonial kindness to the traveller, who traditionally comes to the hearth under the protection of Zeus. Often enough in the poem it is observed that a stranger at the door just might be a god in disguise. Even one of the suitors, more wary than the rest, knows this: 'The gods often disguise themselves as strangers from afar,' he says, 'and move from town to town in

every kind of shape to see whether people are behaving inso-
lently or keeping in good order' (17.485–7).

I can't resist telling at this point the story, rather pointedly
Homeric despite its Celtic concluding line, of the little sister
who looked after the convent portal, instructed by the mother
superior to welcome any visitor who called. 'Bring him in, whoever he is,' the superior would say, 'and treat him kindly. He
could be Saint Joseph.' But one day the little sister went to her
superior to say, 'Mother, there's a man at the door who just
couldn't be Saint Joseph. He's not very well mannered. His
clothes are unkempt. I heard him say a bad word. And I think I
smelled liquor on his breath.' And the mother superior replied,
'Bring him in, whoever he is, and treat him kindly. He could be
Saint Patrick.'

That may not be the kind of hospitality all of us can extend to
anonymous visitors in our troubled Torontos today, but it is still
the kind of Odyssean hospitality you can find in small communi-
ties in Greece. A traveller, however unconventionally dressed, is
treated with almost unbelievable deference. Once in my travels
in Greece I reached an island in the surging sea, and found a
whitewashed hotel that could put me up for one day only, as a
group of prosperous Germans was due to arrive the next day. But
possibly, the proprietor told me politely, a German or two
wouldn't show up with the group, and a bed might still be available for me.

The next day, at rosy-fingered dawn, I went for a long swim
and returned in my swimsuit to the hotel, only to be told that
every last German had arrived, and that I had to vacate my room,
but that perhaps I could find a bed with a family a mile down the
beach; sometimes they put up travellers. But I had better hurry. I
made my way along the loud-sounding sea, and found the humble homestead crowded with merrymakers. The family was having its new baby christened. Everyone, including the bearded
Orthodox *pappas* in his priestly robes, was there, finely dressed,
nor was any heart stinted of the fair feast. When I appeared, an
unclothed stranger at the gate, what was their reaction?

'Come in, come in!' they cried. The reverend *pappas* beckoned
with the piece of bread he had in his hand. There was nothing to

do but accept their hospitality, and I circulated bare-legged and bare-chested among the guests, wine glass in hand. On that sacramental occasion they brought me in and treated me kindly. After all, I could have been Apollo.

The Homeric point in that experience is that, if that family had sent me away, and if in the future anything happened to that baby, someone would surely say, 'Do you remember how, at the christening, that handsome stranger suddenly appeared on the beach, and we didn't offer him hospitality?'

That is a truly Odyssean response. (I might add that there wasn't a room for me at that humble homestead either, and I had to bed down that night in a sleeping bag on the roof of the local church, waiting for the dawn and my black ship back to the mainland.)

I've attempted with some indirection to define the quest, at least as it appears in Homer. And while Virgil, Wagner, and Goethe will add their own details in subsequent chapters, the notion in our four works will remain essentially unchanged. The hero's quest is, at the deepest level, a learning process, a man's search for his inner self. And, as often in the male myth the self and the father are two aspects of the same person, the search for the self is (Goethe perhaps excepted) the search for the father. It is very often a journey from mother to father. But encounters along the way with intuitive, illuminating women are of supreme importance for the hero's discovery of his father and his self. Questing also requires, especially in Homer, acceptance of the rituals of hospitality, without which the travels would be impossible. The quest involves wandering, learning, suffering, even failing, before eventual success. And for this – we're back now where we started – a hero needs strength from sources beyond himself.

All or most of this is summed up by – of all the unexpected and less-than-perceptive figures – Menelaus, in Book 4 of the *Odyssey*. When young Telemachus calls at his palace, the middle-aged war veteran gives the young man, and us, a kind of blueprint for the quest, a miniature version of what, in recent decades, we have come to call, with James Joyce and Joseph Campbell, the monomyth of the hero, the pattern of the figurations that lie at the heart of a hero's questing.

Menelaus says to Telemachus, come to inquire after his father,

'I shall tell you, without hiding or concealing anything, what I heard myself from the infallible lips of the Old Man of the Sea. I was in Egypt, eager to get back home from the Trojan War. The gods kept me there on an island for twenty days. Never in that time did the winds that blow over the deep come to me. Then Eidothea, the daughter of Proteus, the Old Man of the Sea, took pity on me and saved me. She met me as I walking alone, and said, "Sir! Are you an utter fool? Are you weak in the head? Or is it because you *like* hardships that you allow yourself to be marooned all this time on this island?"' (4.348–72)

I'm paraphrasing Homer's Greek and, as you may have spotted by now, I'm availing myself of the idiom of Rieu's Penguin translation – a version too much like Trollope for the taste of Adam Parry,[7] but the version too that has been one of the best-selling paperbacks since the introduction of paperbacks. It has helped make the *Odyssey* of all Greek classics the one most widely read in the English-speaking world. Perhaps at this point Rieu's translation makes Eidothea address the marooned Menelaus as if he were, not a character in Trollope, but the reader of one of the self-help paperbacks that fill our supermarket bookstands. But self-help is what the feminine figure offers in the course of the hero's quest – the self-help that is the way to the discovery of the father.

'Tell me how I can cross the teeming deep,' says Menelaus.

'I will tell you all you need to know,' Eidothea replies. 'This island is the haunt of the old man of the sea, the infallible Proteus, who knows the ocean in all its depths. He is, I'm told, the father who begot me.'

The island, by the way, is called Pharos. One day a wondrous *pharos*, a lighthouse, would bring illumination to Egypt's sea. The father-figure is associated with light, and often with the sun. He is in most myths uncommonly elusive as well. So Eidothea says,

'When the sun has reached mid-heaven, Proteus comes out of the sea, hidden by the black ripples made by the West Wind, and lies down to sleep in the shelter of a cave, with the flippered seals in herds around him ... Choose three of your comrades, and I will lead you there and find each of you a place to lie. Directly you see him settled down to sleep, summon all your strength and courage and hold him fast, however hard he strains and struggles to escape. He will change himself into every shape that creeps upon the earth, and into water too, and blazing fire. But hold him fast. And ask him how you may cross the teeming deep, and come home.' (4.400–24)

And with that she disappears into the sea. A nymph of the water, that prime symbol of the feminine unconscious, she probably knows herself the reason for Menelaus's being delayed on the island, for in Jungian terms Eidothea represents Menelaus's anima – his intuitive feminine side. She tells him 'all he needs to know' in the practical order. But a male hero encountering his anima eventually must be granted deeper illumination from that other archetype in the psyche, the fatherly Wise Old Man, who, in Homer's scenario, emerges from the intuitive waters when the sun is blazing at high noon.

So it is that, in the mist of morning, Eidothea comes with four seal skins, and covers Menelaus and his three comrades with them. The skins are, amusingly, foul-smelling: 'I should like to know,' says Menelaus via Rieu, 'who would choose a monster of the deep for a bed-fellow!' (4.443). That is as close as Menelaus ever comes to saying (perhaps it is as close as he ever comes to realizing) that the reason for his finding himself becalmed in Egypt, awaiting illumination on the isle of Pharos, is that he must, before he returns home from the Trojan War, come to terms with the bed-fellow he is, after ten years, bringing back with him.

How *did* Helen and Menelaus forgive each other when the Trojan War was over? How did *he* come to terms with her faithlessness, and *she* with his vindictiveness? It is a question that has preoccupied poets and dramatists from Stesichorus and Euripides to Goethe in *Faust* to Richard Strauss and Hugo von Hofmannsthal in their opera *Die Aegyptische Helena*. In that piece, written after the First World War, Menelaus returning with Helen 'is cured of his war neuroses ... by acting out his inner feelings.'[8]

The situation becomes, in the psychologizing way of early-twentieth-century opera, a story of what we have since come to call the male mid-life crisis. But the quasi-psychiatric libretto by the Viennese poet, for all its wealth of strange figures and symbols, doesn't provide the simple archetypes that one finds in Book 4 of the *Odyssey*. Homer's blueprint gives us the very figures that Jung discovered in the psyches of the middle-aged Menelauses who came to him in Zurich: a man is helped by his anima to find his Wise Old Man and his self. Homer is, as always, simpler and subtler than the artists who follow him, and more perceptive.

The practical Eidothea makes the stench of the sealskins bearable by applying ambrosia to each man's nostrils. Then Proteus comes from the sea to sleep under the flaming sun. (Virgil, in his version of this tale in the fourth book of his *Georgics*, stresses even more than Homer does the fiery heat of the sun when the Wise Old Man appears.) Menelaus and his companions make the most of the mid-day moment. They rush from hiding and pin Proteus down, despite the frightening archetypal shapes – water and fire – he assumes. And Proteus finally tells Menelaus that he has been arrested in his journey because (it is the very first point we made) he has not acknowledged the divine aid the hero must acknowledge on his quest. He has not made the sacrifices necessary for his return. He must sail up the Nile once more and perform them. Then he will be given passage home. And, when the time comes for him to die, he will be transported to the Elysium at the earth's end, 'where falls not hail nor rain nor any snow / nor ever wind blows loudly.'[9] There he will live forever because – he was Helen's husband.

This story, told near the beginning of the *Odyssey* by a Menelaus who may or may not know its full import, is in outline the story of the *Odyssey* to follow. It is a paradigm of the quest of the hero to find – with the help of his inner feminine and his inner masculine, his Eidothea and his Proteus, the water and the fire of his soul – the self that is the completion of his odyssey. And in the *Odyssey* that self will eventually be found in the hero's loving union with his wife. His bedfellow will be immortality for Menelaus, fulfilment for Odysseus.

Let us turn at last to Odysseus himself, and his encounters with the archetypes.

First, the anima-figures. Often in myth the feminine anima attempts to arrest the hero on his quest; often she attempts to destroy him. The ultimate challenge for Odysseus in his adventure-flashbacks are the monsters Scylla and Charybdis – Scylla with savage dogs barking at her groin, and Charybdis drawing defenceless ships down in her swirling vortex. These two figures, with their obvious sexual aspects, represent the traditional fear a hero has of the feminine.

Two other fearsome females are the Sirens. In popular imagination the Sirens are the very image of the dangers of eroticism. Not so in Homer, who has in Scylla and Charybdis more than enough of that. Homer's Sirens promise Odysseus not sexual pleasure but knowledge: 'Come! Come! We know all that happens on this fruitful earth.' Possibly for an ordinary sailor the Sirens might sing a song that promises erotic satisfactions, but Odysseus is no ordinary sailor. For him the Sirens extend the promise of endless intellectual questing. (Perhaps Homer's Sirens should be thought to sing a song appropriate to the desires of each man who passes. Were I to pass the Sirens' island, they'd very likely sing, 'We know all the archetypal operas that Mozart would have written had he lived past the age of thirty-five. We can sing you, not just his *Magic Flute*, but his *Faust*, his *Parsifal*, his *Aeneid*, his *Odyssey*.' I'd likely leap overboard at that temptation.)

In any case, it is characteristic of the anima, when it cannot utterly destroy the hero, to attempt by any means it can to arrest his onward journey. And yet the anima, potentially destructive, proves, when its destructive aspect is defeated, to be creative and helpful. And here we must pause to consider something quite unique in the voyaging of Homer's hero.

In most hero myths, the way to the anima is, as we remarked in our first chapter, prepared for by an encounter with a male figure, quite the opposite of the hero, which Jung calls the shadow. Odysseus is not companioned by such a figure.[10] Neither is Menelaus in the blueprint of the hero's journey in Book 4. Perhaps this is the case because Odysseus and Menelaus are mature men. (The inexperienced and fatherless Telemachus is in his maturing companioned by a kind of shadow, Peisistratus, an experienced lad his own age who has had proper fathering from Nestor.)

But when the mature Odysseus makes a voyage beyond anything he has experienced, the voyage to the Underworld in Book 11, he does encounter a shadow-figure in Elpenor, the young sailor who, in a drunken stupor, has fallen from Circe's roof, broken his neck, and passed – an unburied shade – to Hades. The hapless and helpless Elpenor is, as a shadow-figure must be, quite the opposite of the mature and self-possessed hero. And, as Odysseus discloses when he tells his adventure tales to the royal court at Phaeacia, Elpenor is the first figure he meets among the dead. Wary at first of the shadow, Odysseus draws his sword and faces Elpenor across the pool of sacrificial blood that has allowed him his vision of the afterlife. But Elpenor only pleads for proper burial, and Odysseus, befriending his shadow, promises to grant him that as his due.

This leads immediately to the hero's Underworld encounter with the anima, in the form of his dead mother, Anticleia. Odysseus has been warned that the anima/mother may attempt to arrest him, so, with sword still drawn, he does not speak to the figure, or allow it to drink of the blood and so speak to him, until he has encountered – once again, immediately – his Wise Old Man archetype in the person of the prophet Teiresias. Only after he hears the old man's mysterious words about and instructions for his future does the hero speak to the ghost of his mother, who tells him, helpfully as always with the tamed anima, what he must know practically about the present state of Ithaca, the goal of his questing. And once his mother has spoken, the queen of the underworld, Persephone, sends upwards, in a dazzling array of anima-figures, the mothers of virtually every Greek hero in the mythological canon.

So impressed by this confirmation of the anima's power is the powerful womanly listener to this tale, Queen Arete of Phaeacia, that she, who till this moment had seemed antagonistic to the hero, calls on her Phaeacians to escort him on a magic ship across the sea to Ithaca. (And, quite expectedly, her amiable husband concurs in this.)

In the course of the adventure books, Odysseus meets a whole succession of such potentially destructive, potentially helpful, and even motherly anima-figures: Circe, 'the hawk' who has the power to turn him into a beast but, when he defeats her destructive aspect in a symbolic battle of the sexes, gives him new clothes and provides him with the means to make his journey to the world of the dead; Calypso, the 'veiled one' who, after a thousand nights of love, cannot keep him forever on her quasi-Tahitian island, even with the promise of immortality, and who finally clothes him and speeds him on his way; Leucothoe, the 'white wave' who might have submerged him but who rises bird-like from the sea to give him the veil that takes him, otherwise naked and defenceless, through the worst storm the sea can send; Nausicaa, the young Phaeacian 'lady of the ships,' who, in the freshest exchange of dialogue in all the literature I have read, responds to Odysseus as in his nakedness he pleads with her, who clothes him and saves him and then wisely decides it would be better to live in his memory than to share his life with him; and finally Nausicaa's mother, queen Arete, 'she who is prayed to,' who spins sea-purple webs on her island on the border between fairy-land and reality, who sees beyond the hero's clothes and his fabrications, and finally provides him, blanketed and sleeping, with passage by magic ship to his homeland.

What we have here, as has been remarked with increasing frequency in recent years,[11] is a galaxy of luminous ladies who clothe the hero and lead him onward, in a series of tests, toward the eventual discovery of his self in the arms of his wife, the veiled Penelope. The name Penelope may mean, from *pene* and *olopto*, 'she who plucks the thread,' and of course Penelope is famous for deceiving the suitors by that ruse.[12] But I would rather derive her name, as is also possible, from *pene* and *opsis*, that is to say 'she with the thread across her face.' Penelope first appears, in Book 1, 'drawing a shining veil across her cheeks' (1.334). And she veils her face again when at 18.210–13 she appears in all her loveliness to the suitors, and (nowhere is her likeness to Circe so pronounced) their limbs are loosed and their hearts maddened with love, and each of them prays that he might sleep with her. Most of the time Penelope weeps, but when Athene puts her to sleep to prepare her for that appearance before the suitors (and before the man who is her husband in disguise), Penelope, for one wonderful moment, laughs. We cannot say at that point why she does so, and why in another few lines she impulsively passes her hands before her face.[13] She remains, through almost the whole of the last half of the poem, mysterious. We do not know, from book to book, how much she knows about the unkempt hero who comes in disguise to her gate, into her courtyard, and into her chambers. We only know that, until the moment when she chooses to accept that stranger as her husband, she remains inscrutable and – in effect if not always in fact – veiled.

The ladies encountered on the way to Penelope may be thought to be so many veils of Penelope: Calypso's name means 'veil'; Leucothoe lends the hero her veil; Arete and Circe, like Penelope, spin webs at their looms. Then, the last half of the *Odyssey*, the hero's experience when he returns alone and unknown to his kingdom, is like the lifting of a series of veils.[14] At first Odysseus, set ashore blanketed and sleeping, cannot recognize his own island when he wakes – not till Athene lifts the veil of mist she has cast over it. Then, disguised by Athene as a ragged beggar, Odysseus enters into his rightful roles one by one, revealing himself as a father to Telemachus (Book 16), as a master to his dog (Book 17), as the child she had once nursed to Eurycleia (Book 19), as protector to his servants (Book 21), as avenging king to the suitors (Book 22), and as husband to Penelope (Book 23). The last half of the *Odyssey* is a wonderful series of recognition scenes, of veils lifted.

In one of these, Telemachus's 'little quest,' which has developed in artful stages along with his father's larger tale, reaches its climax. This recognition scene between father and son in Book 16 is as poignant, as carefully protracted, as any in Greek tragedy. Odysseus, in his beggar's disguise, has had the opportunity to observe Telemachus quietly, in the hut of his swineherd. He sees, in those humble surroundings, that his son is a good son – princely, courteous, hospitable, and, like himself, wary. Finally, the two are alone.

Athene, visible only to Odysseus, touches him with her wand.

His heroic figure and kingly clothing are, for a moment, restored to him. After nineteen years, the son sees his father.

'Stranger,' the young man cries in fear and amazement (or – in Homer's famous phrase – with winged words), 'You are not the same now as you were! You are one of the gods! Have mercy on me.'[15]

'I am no god,' Odysseus says, 'I am your father.' He kisses his son, and a tear rolls down his cheek to the ground – though till now with his son he has held his tears back.

'You are *not* my father,' the boy cries.

Odysseus replies, 'Telemachus, do not wonder overmuch that your father is here with you at last. I am Odysseus, returned to my own country. This change you see is the work of the goddess Athene, who makes of me whatever she wills' (16.181–212).

At that Telemachus flings his arms around his father's neck, and they weep for the years they have lost. They cry aloud like – Homer says in one of the most startling of his similes – sea-eagles, or like vultures with twisted talons, when villagers have robbed their nest of their unfledged young. Why, at this moment when father and son have at last found each other, a comparison to birds who lament that their young have been lost? Surely because father and son are weeping for the years they have lost, years when they might have come to know each other.[16] Then why, at this tender moment, a comparison to, of all birds, the sea-eagle or the vulture? Because the passage is too important to be sentimentalized. The wary, sea-sailing Odysseus, whom his wife will see in a dream as an eagle, must be kept in character. And Telemachus's quest will not be completed until, at his father's side, he visits, with winged arrows, due punishment – death, in fact – on the suitors.

The supreme recognition scene, however – and I can't think of any in Greek tragedy that compares in subtlety with this one – is the scene in Book 23 with Penelope, the climax of Odysseus's quest.

There is a critical problem with Penelope. Her words and actions in Books 19 to 23 can be read in more than one way. In my teaching days I used to reread *The Turn of the Screw* before attempting to teach Books 17 to 23 of the *Odyssey*, for Henry

James in his twisting, ambivalent ghost story invites us to consider two possibilities. In the usual reading, the little boy and girl at Bly are possessed by evil spirits, and the governess, attempting to save the children, destroys them. But in another reading, made familiar through the play and film adaptation called *The Innocents*, the children are innocent; the governess reads her own neuroses into them, and in trying to save them destroys them. Either reading can be derived from the ingenious framing and construction of the story. And just as the reader thinks he has things sorted out, James will give the situation another turn of the screw, and the reader is forced to reconsider his reading.

Some Homerists, following the old German analytic tradition, have seen the second part of the *Odyssey* as deriving from two or more separate traditions, now lost to us, in which the character and motives of Penelope varied considerably.[17] I don't think that this can be proved from the poem as we have it. What we can say is that the poem as we have it has a fine sense of Jamesian ambivalence. When Odysseus finally returns to his Ithaca in disguise, and bides his time before revealing himself to Penelope, we who read are invited to wonder, through book after book, 'What's going on in her head? How much does she know about the stranger in her house? How much does *he* know she knows? How much does *she* know he knows she knows?' Answers vary,[18] but with every new turn of the screw, my answer is, '*He* may begin to suspect at some point that she knows who he is, but *she* knows who he is from the start.' She laughs at the prospect of appearing beautiful before him and impulsively passes her hands before the face she knows will be veiled, so that he will not know how much she knows. Women, in this poem, are more perceptive than men.

Penelope is the fulfilment of all of Odysseus's encounters with women who seek to know his identity. All of the anima-figures are preparatory to her. When the powerful queen Arete had seen that Odysseus was dressed in clothes from her own palace, and asked him, *tis pothen eis andrōn* ('Who are you? Where are you from?'), and when the fearful Circe, impressed by Odysseus's resistance to her power, asked him, again, *tis pothen eis andrōn*, they clearly did not know who he was. But when Penelope asks him the selfsame *tis pothen eis andrōn*, at their first tentative meeting by her illuminating fireside, I feel that, though he is dressed in a beggar's rags, she knows, and knows full well, who he is. For by hints and tokens, by the memory of the clothes she once gave him, and especially – we are not surprised by this – by telling him of a dream she has had, she convinces him that he should proceed with the secret plan he has in his head: he must destroy the suitors. 'In my dream,' she says, 'I saw a great eagle swoop down and kill all the geese in my palace. Then the eagle broke into speech and said to me, "Take heart. This is not a dream, but a reality you shall see fulfilled. The geese were your suitors, and I, who played the eagle's part, I am your husband, returned home and ready to deal out punishment to them all"' (19.536–50).

I said at the start that sleep, and the revelations that come in sleep, are of some importance in the *Odyssey*. Telemachus making decisive plans under his blanket in Book 1 is the nicest image in Homer for consciousness emerging from the unconscious. And it is the first of a pattern. At the beginning of Book 20, on the night before the action in Ithaca reaches its climax, the disguised Odysseus, tossing restlessly under his sheepskin in the courtyard, is assured by Athene that he will come through the evils that beset him,[19] and is then put soundly to sleep. At that very moment Penelope wakes in her bedroom with the premonition, after a dream, that he has been near her in the night. Then, at dawn, he lying below hears her weeping in the room above, and he seems to see her standing by his head, fully aware of who he is. His morning prayer to Zeus is answered by a bolt of thunder. This is heard by an old slave woman working through the night, and that woman's prayer – that the suitors who have enslaved her be punished – is communicated to Odysseus, and gives him strength.

In short, there is a kind of psychic communication at work in the *Odyssey* – between Odysseus and Telemachus when they are separated by stretches of land and sea,[20] between Odysseus and the old slave woman as the day of victory dawns, and especially between Odysseus and Penelope through the night – and the bed is the intuitive place whereby the communications pass. Odysseus is conveyed home on a Phaeacian ship sleeping and blanketed; Penelope sleeps all through the horrors of the battle with the suitors, 'the sweetest and soundest sleep since Odysseus left for Troy.' Small wonder that it is the bed they share that provides the resolution for this intricate and beautiful poem.

We come at last to that resolution.

A mythic hero finds, at the end of his quest, a sign that he has found himself at the centre of all he has learned. A sign of the self. The terminology is, again, Jung's, and for Jung it is often expressed in such centripetal designs as, to use his favourite sign, the mandala. At the end of the quest, the parts of the hero's life come together harmoniously in an indivisible circular symbol.

When the suitors are slain, and Odysseus's terrible work is done, he tells Penelope his name and hopes to be welcomed at last in her embrace. But she quietly refuses to recognize him, even when he returns to her freshly bathed and clothed and 'certain that he is irresistable now.'[21] This is the last of his learning experiences, and the most challenging of them all, for Penelope uses his own tricks, his famous lies, against him. She announces that she will not sleep with a man who is not her husband, and asks the nurse Eurycleia to move her husband's bed outside for this stranger, implying not only that she does not believe him, but that her husband's bed was, like any other bed, replaceable.

'Who,' Odysseus asks, more I think in panic than in indignation, 'who has moved my bed?'

'There is no man alive, be he ever so young and strong, who could pry it from its place. A great sign went into the making of that bed. It was my work and mine alone. Inside my court there was a long-leaved olive tree, which had grown to full height, with a stem as thick as a pillar. Round this I built my bedchamber, till I had it finished, with thick-set stones. I roofed it over and put in a solid double door. I lopped off all the twigs from the tree, and trimmed the stem from the root up, and rounded it smoothly and carefully with an adze and trued it to the line, to make my bedpost. I bored through the whole of it with an augur, and I hewed out my bed till it was finished, with an inlay of gold, silver, and ivory. And I stretched over it an oxhide, bright with purple.' (23.187–201)

'There,' he says to his wife, 'is my sign.'

There, Jung would say, is his mandala.

The bed of this hero and his wife was to be, like their union, immovable and permanent. Odysseus's whole house has been patterned around it. So he is confounded at the thought, not only that he must sleep alone after his final victory, but that his most intimate secret has been disclosed, that the privacy, the permanence of his existence has been disrupted and destroyed. That moment in Book 23 is the only point in the poem where the wily hero is at a loss for wiles, and it may properly be regarded as the point to which all the adventures and revelations have been leading. It also points up beautifully the complementary natures of man and woman, at least of this man and this woman: once long before, *he* had wept like a woman who clings to the body of her dead husband (8.523–31); now (23.233–40) *she* clings to him like a sailor who, covered with brine, emerges from a stormy sea.[22] With that very Odyssean simile Penelope accepts her Odysseus. And she accepts him not because she is sure at last of his identity (that she had surely known long before), but because at last she is in a position to tell him who he is. She alone of all the figures in the many recognition scenes reverses the revelation and confers his name, his self, upon him. And one of the nicest touches in Homer is that her knees are trembling as she does so.

It's a wise child who knows his own father and, as Charles Rowan Beye puts it, writing *finis* to the *Odyssey*'s two quests, 'a wiser man who finds his own wife.'[23] But could the wise Odysseus ever have ended his quest, and come home to his wife and his bed, without aid from a source beyond himself? He has divine aid from – how could we have delayed our consideration of her so long? – from Athene, the very goddess of wisdom, the bright personage who, like Goethe's 'Eternal Feminine,' leads the hero onwards. In the theogonic order of things, Athene sprang full-grown from the brain of Zeus. She is the feminine embodiment of the father god's wisdom, integrating human feminine and masculine principles in her one luminous person – as the hero himself must learn to do. She too may be thought a symbol of the completed quest. She is not with Odysseus in his adventures at sea, out of what she calls deference to Uncle Poseidon and what we see as the hero's passage through his own psyche. But when he returns from those fantastic encounters to the practical concerns of kingship, she is his guide again: 'Here I am once more, to weave a plan with you ... I cannot desert you. You are so civilized, so intelligent, so self-possessed' (13.303, 331–2).

Athene helps the son on his 'little quest' for his father at the start of the poem, and at its end she helps them both. When in Book 19 father and son begin to map out together their vengeance on the suitors, removing the armour from the great hall, Athene raises a golden lamp and leads the way for them. The feminine emblem of male reason, she carries aloft the symbol of male consciousness – fire. 'Look, father,' says the rapidly maturing boy. 'The walls, the panels, the pine-wood beams, the soaring pillars all stand out as though there were a blazing fire. Some god is in the house.'

'Hush!' Odysseus cautions. 'The Olympians have ways of their own. Off to bed now' (19.36–44).

A few centuries later, an Athenian artist sculpted the 'dreaming Athena' that most suggests the goddess's bright presence in Homer. And an unknown Greek writing in Egypt, speaking at times in the person of Solomon, described wisdom itself as a woman, 'intelligent, holy, unique, manifold, subtle, agile ... mobile beyond all motion ... an arm of the might of God and a pure effusion of his glory.'[24] That sounds like Homer's Athene.

Now here is a thought that occurs to many readers of the *Odyssey*: is the presence in the poem of the goddess of wisdom somehow the idea of Penelope always operative in Odysseus's mind? The Egyptian Greek writing *The Book of Wisdom* goes on to say:

Her I loved and sought often from my youth. I sought to take her for my bride, and became a lover of her beauty. She understands the subtleties of phrases and the solution of riddles; signs and wonders she knows in advance, and the outcome of times and ages. So I determined to take her to live with me, knowing that she would be my counsellor ... Within my dwelling, I should take my repose beside her, thinking this within myself and reflecting in my heart, that there is immortality in kinship with wisdom.

Have you nodded off? Because at long last, lit by blazing torches, with soft blankets and due ceremony, Odysseus and Penelope go happily to the bedchamber that is theirs and theirs alone. Some critics – famous Homerists from Aristarchus and Aristophanes of Byzantium to Wilamowitz, Denys Page, and G.S. Kirk – hold that the *Odyssey* ends there, at line 296 in Book 23. We are to think of the rest as a series of additions made by inferior hands at the lyre. But for many of us it is still the real Homer who goes on for another page to tell us, with his usual discretion, that love took its sweet course for Odysseus and Penelope, and that they turned then to the delights of – this is surely Homeric! – the delights of talk. Homer says that *she* tells him of all she has suffered at home, and then *he* tells her about the Cyclops and Circe and the Underworld and the Sirens. As they lie in their olive-tree bed, she hears (though the stories are not recounted for us) how Calypso provided poplars and firs for his raft; how an olive tree grown together with a thorn bush sheltered him when, shipwrecked, he crawled ashore to sleep in Phaeacia;[25] how Nausicaa, when she rescued him there, looked – or at least he flattered her that she looked – like a young palm tree at Delos; how a staff of green olive wood, pointed and set afire, saved him from Polyphemus; how the magical plant *mōly* saved him from Circe; how a high-perched fig tree saved him from Charybdis, and how, finally, a long-leaved olive tree welcomed him, and guarded his treasure, when he came home to Ithaca. And just as he finishes his last tale, sleep comes suddenly on him. What could be more Odyssean? Love, winged words, sheltering trees, and sleep.

There is less authority for Homeric authorship of the last book, which is, I must admit, a sometimes inept attempt, almost surely by various hands, to tie loose ends together.[26] We might expect the author or authors of the last book to concern themselves with the ultimate journey enjoined on the hero: wise old Teiresias told him from the world of the dead that when he finally came home he had to take a well-cut oar and proceed inland until he came to a place where people never use salt with their food and know nothing of the sea or of ships – that is to say, far, far away from Poseidon's influence, so far in fact that Odysseus will meet a stranger who, seeing the oar he carries, will ask why he has a winnowing fan on his shoulder. There, Teiresias told him, he had to plant the oar in the earth, sacrifice to Poseidon, and return home to await a gentle death out of the sea, surrounded by his prosperous people.

It might have made a wonderful last book, but it is not what we have been given in Homer's Book 24. Still, there is one passage in Book 24 so moving, so germane to my purposes in this book, and so appropriate to one of the patterns of imagery we have traced, that I must cite it in closing.

Odysseus has re-established himself as king, master, father, and husband. He has assumed every one of his old roles except that of son. Some Homeric bard rightly thought that the poem needed one last recognition scene. The hero who has found his self has also to find his father. (Similarly, whatever bard completed the *Iliad* ended that poem too with the hero remembering his father, and finding release at last from the passion that possessed him.)

So, in the *Odyssey*'s last book, Odysseus finds his father and, in a wonderful recognition scene, releases him from the malady that has possessed him. He finds Laertes old and poorly clothed, head down, hoeing round a plant in his orchard. The hero halts behind a pear tree, wondering whether to run to his father and kiss him or whether, as in every other such scene in the *Odyssey*, to question him. He decides on the latter course. I do not believe, with some others, that his action here is cruel. I believe that the old man has, in the long absence of his son, gone mad. And that the son must now use questions to lead his father gradually, firmly, out of his madness:[27]

'Old man, you have everything so tidy here. I can see that there is little about gardening that you do not know. There is nothing, not a green thing in the whole enclosure, not a fig tree or a vine, not an olive or a pear tree, not a garden plot that does not show signs of your care.'
(24.244–247)

The work old Laertes has done is a characteristic response for a desperate man whose life is in disorder – he has kept a hold on sanity by working at something he *can* put in order.

Odysseus continues: 'On the other hand – and do not take offence at this – you do not look after *yourself* very well ... You might be a man of royal blood. Tell me. Who is your master? Whose orchard do you tend?'

No response.

'Tell me this. Am I really in Ithaca? A fellow I met on my way here assured me that I was. But he was not very intelligent, and he would not even listen to me.'

No response.

'Some time ago I entertained a stranger who said he was from Ithaca, and that Laertes was his father. I took him into my house and gave him hospitality.'

Something quickens in the old man.

'Sir,' he says, coming out of his trauma, with tears in his eyes, 'that guest of yours was my unhappy son, as sure as ever such a man there was. So tell me this and tell me true: *tis pothen eis andrōn*?'

Odysseus proceeds, as he does elsewhere in the poem, with a string of elaborate lies. But for once, he uses the lies, not to protect himself in a potentially hostile world, but to keep the revelation of himself to his father steady, tactful, healing. The last of the lies, when he is sure that the old man is ready for it, is, 'Odysseus left my country pursued by an evil fate – and yet the omens he left with were good ones, and I rejoiced in them as I sent him on his way. He ventured forth happily. Both our hearts hoped that we two should meet again.'

So Odysseus forces his old father to face the feelings he has so long repressed. When Laertes picks up the black dust in both his hands and pours it over his head, and weeps, Odysseus knows that the shell of his father's orderly insanity has been broken at last. He seizes the moment, rushes forward, clasps his father and kisses him. 'Father, here I am. I have come home.'

But of course the heroic quest requires that the encounter with the evasive old man result in personal illumination for the quester. Laertes is now aware enough to demand proof. He is like any number of tough-minded old men I've met on Greek islands.

Odysseus shows the scar on his thigh.

Not enough.

Odysseus tells his father the name of *his* father, Autolycus.

Not enough.

Then Odysseus finds the right thing to say:

'I will tell you all the trees you gave me one day on this very terrace. I was only a little boy at the time, trotting after you through the orchard, begging for this one and that one, and as we wound our way through these orderly rows you told me all their names. You gave me thirteen pear-, ten apple-, and forty fig-trees, and at the same time you pointed out the fifty rows of vines that were to be mine. Each ripened at a different time, so that the bunches on them were at various stages when the seasons of Zeus weighed them down from above.' (24.336–44)

Trees set in rows – the perfect image for the mazes of memory, the permanence of nature, the continuity of the family. The reader who is attentive to Homeric undercurrents will perhaps remember at this point a simile from Book 5, when after two days and two nights in the sea the shipwrecked Odysseus finally sights land from the crest of a wave:

As to his children there comes as a blessing the recovery of a father who lies in sickness, bearing harsh pains for many years and wasting away (for some cruel spirit has him in its grip) and then the gods blessedly free him from his malady, so to Odysseus there came as a blessing the sight of the land and the trees. (5.394–8)

There in the orchard old Laertes, with trembling knees and bursting heart, flings his arms around his son, and Odysseus catches him fainting to his breast. That is the image from Homer I'd like to leave you with, until we talk more about heroes, fathers, trees, sufferings, and completed quests in Virgil, in the next chapter.

CHAPTER THREE

The Golden Bough

The cave of the Sibyl at Cumae, destroyed by Byzantine and Saracen armies, abandoned for a thousand years, and unearthed by Amedeo Maiuri only in 1932, is one archaeological site that does not disappoint the traveller, though a casual reader of Virgil might be led to expect something different from what can actually be seen at Cumae today.[1] Virgil says, near the beginning of Book 6 of the *Aeneid*:

Into the massive flank of the rock was carved a cave. A hundred wide entrances and a hundred doors lead into it, and out of it rush one hundred voices – the oracular responses of the Sibyl. (6.42–4)

You might visualize, reading that, a wall of rock perforated with as many apertures as pierce the Marabar hills in E.M. Forster's *A Passage to India*. You would at least expect to find at Cumae some sort of labyrinthine complex. But Virgil is famous – some would say notorious – for his blending of various descriptive details into mysterious, almost impressionistic wholes.[2] What one finds today in the cave at Cumae is a single, 431-foot long, 16-foot high, trapezoidally (almost triangularly) shaped passage cut into a cliff of yellow tufa, widening at the far end into a triple chamber – the vaulted adyton where the Sibyl once sat enthroned, singing her responses. The long dark cavern is sectioned into six successive chambers, each of them illuminated by daylight from a fenestration cut laterally in the right, or seaward, wall. Marks at the sides of each chamber still indicate where there were hinges for the doors.

Virgil's 'hundred corridors and doors' is his poet's way of conveying the impression that would have been made on a solitary questioner when, overawed, he stood in the darkness at the cave's single entrance and saw, facing him, door after door flung open and, in each successive chamber, a flash of bright daylight piercing the darkness sideways – and when he heard, with each flash of light, the high-pitched wail from the adyton at the far end coming clearer and clearer. It was a cry that told him of himself and of his future. (You'll remember how the echo in the Marabar caves affected the futures of Forster's terrified ladies, Mrs Moore and Miss – note the name – Miss Quested.)

Virgil's art is vastly different from Homer's. His *Aeneid* has nothing like the descriptive clarity, the almost tangible objectivity, that Erich Auerbach so admired in the *Odyssey*. But the *Aeneid* may be thought to ask, through the obscure language of prophecy, larger questions than Homer asks. On his first page, or rather at the start of his first scroll, Virgil asks the Muses two of the great human questions: 'What is God?' and 'If God is good, why do the innocent suffer?' That is the way I read his characteristically elusive phrases *tantaene animis caelestibus irae?* ('Can there be so much wrath in the power on high?') and *tot volvere casus / insignem pietate virum?* ('... to whirl through so many disasters a man famous for his devotion to duty').

Virgil's concept of the power that rules the universe is not the mythological pantheon familiar from Homer's epics, even though, writing as he is in an epic tradition, he uses many of the Olympian figures for narrative and symbolic purposes.[3] The notion of divinity that pervades his epic, memorably stated in a passage in his earlier *Georgics* (4.219–27), is rather the Stoic concept of one god, an intelligence that rules the world for ultimate good and imbues its chosen heroes with a 'divine spark.'[4] As Tennyson put it, Virgil's view was one of 'universal Nature moved by universal Mind.'[5] But Tennyson rightly sensed as well that in the *Aeneid* Virgil had become 'majestic in [his] sadness at the doubtful doom of humankind': in the world ruled by a provident god there is unexplainable evil and suffering.[6] The two great questions on the *Aeneid*'s first page remain unanswered on the last page because Virgil has found no answers to them. His hero receives only partial answers when he visits Cumae and the cave of the Sibyl and, with her aid, journeys below the earth to find his dead father.

Virgil would almost certainly have visited Cumae himself, for the villa where he wrote some of the *Georgics* and all of the *Aeneid* was not far away, in what is now Posillipo (where Wagner was to write some of *Parsifal*). In Virgil's day Cumae was a crowded place, a newly re-established religious centre and a busy military base. Virgil had to use his shifting, equivocal techniques to conjure up, for his epic purposes, the land of mystery Cumae might have been when his hero went there, twelve centuries earlier.

When we visit the site today, twenty centuries later, we actually see a more mysterious Cumae than Virgil did. I went to Cumae once. Not (as might have happened had fate not intervened) on a conducted tour with a group from the Villa Vergiliana. My father's death had changed those plans in the summer of 1965. So my impressions of Cumae are nowhere near so exact as the careful descriptions to be found in the written reports of my friends Professor Sandy McKay and the late Father Raymond Schoder. My impressions are formed from a solitary visit made to the site in the autumn of 1974, without guide or guidebook. It was almost ten years after my father's death ended my initial, more scholarly plan that I found myself venturing at last, alone and as a mere pilgrim, to Virgil's Cumae – to the area formed by the eruption of a vast volcano some thirty-five thousand years ago.

I began my journey to Cumae among the crowds in downtown Naples, asking directions from an outlandishly uniformed policeman – a big, handsome fellow, mustachioed, helmeted, and plumed.

'Where can I find the Stazione Ferroviaria Cumana?'

'*Oh si, signore. Ferroviaria Cumana, si!*' he smiled. 'The station is up that street. Straight ahead. But, signore,' he added without any change of expression, 'I wouldn't go up there if I were you. *Molto pericoloso.* Very ... ah ... dangerous.'

Remembering that Naples had for almost a century resigned itself to chaotic and dangerous living (*Vedi Napoli e poi muori* – 'See Naples and die' – has in our era taken on a whole new meaning), I made my way cautiously up the strepitous street.

'Look out for pickpockets,' the carabiniere shouted after me with a friendly but unhelpful wave of his gloved hand.

Possibly the pickpockets heard him. I found the station *senza incidente* and, though the man at the ticket window looked at me dubiously, I promptly boarded the nondescript train, only to find that it proceeded mostly underground and went in the direction of, but not very near to, Cumae. But could I object to that? Virgil's hero had faced many dangers reaching Cumae too, and had gone underground when he got there.

The intermittent view from the screeching subterranean *diretto* – grimy walls from grimy windows – was unpoetic but suitably hellish. One of the underground stops was actually called by the name Greeks and Romans long before Virgil had given the area – the flaming fields. 'Perhaps,' I thought to myself when I saw that name through my underground window, 'I should get off here.' I'd been told that at the Campi Flegrei you can still see an expanse of small sulphurous pits burning and bubbling over, and easily imagine an area once pock-marked with larger volcanic craters and suffused with smoky flames. But I didn't get off. I clanked on under- and overground, wondering if I was doing this right.

I ascended to the upper air at Fusaro and waited for the local autobus, eyed with suspicion by the local inhabitants. Eventually the bus lumbered up late, and took me several miles, slowly enough, till it came to the point nearest to the ancient site. I disembarked. The biggest thing there was the sky.

I turned back to the driver. 'Now, when I want to return,' I asked, 'do I get the autobus at this same place?'

He pushed his cap back by the visor and smiled laconically. '*Oh no, signore. Sciopero.*' And he and his bus were off in a cloud of dust.

Sciopero! Here I was alone in the middle of Virgil's volcanic nowhere, in bandit country, in changeable weather – and the busses were going on strike.

There was nothing to do but visit Cumae first and then worry. From the road, I could see in the distance the abrupt eminence that still remained from the rim of the vast prehistoric crater, the first place where, in the ages of history, Greeks had settled in Italy. The sun climbed as I started across the horizontal landscape. The wind from the sea kept me cool.

So we begin our second consideration together – the quest in Virgil's *Aeneid*. And we shall consider mainly the part of the hero-myth that, in Homer, we dealt with only briefly – the hero's descent to the world of the dead. Book 6 of the *Aeneid* is the one book in which Virgil may safely be said to have surpassed his predecessor. It is famous for its mythic aspects, for it is clearly a descent into the hero's psyche. But it is also heavy with history. Virgil worked, as Professor Robson told us many times back in 1951,[7] in a tradition of written epic, something to be carefully distinguished from Homer's oral epic. Homer *sang* in a century we cannot name, perhaps at the behest of a ruler or of rulers we do not know. Virgil *wrote* at a pivotal moment in recorded history, perhaps at the behest, and certainly with the encouragement,[8] of a ruler we know very well – Caesar Augustus. In that penultimate decade BC Augustus was the most powerful man in the world, and Virgil's hero Aeneas, leading a remnant of Trojans out of their fallen city across the sea to a new land won by new wars, can be and has often been seen as a figure for that powerful man, the young Octavian who came to be called Augustus,[9] leading his Romans from a ruined republic through a succession of wars to an empire yet to be built.

I shall return to Augustus before this chapter is done. But first let us volve the Virgil scroll as far as the sixth book, which in my memory is very much the Robson book, and briefly tell the story of the *Aeneid* to that point in terms of its key words – fate, fury, and piety.

Trojan Aeneas, *fato profugus*, driven on by fate, has arrived at last in Italy. He is a man who has always been known among Trojans for his *pietas*, his devotion to duty. And yet, fleeing from the destruction of his city, he has been opposed, and will continue to be opposed at every turn, by the *furor*, the wrath, of the goddess Juno. Till now he has been given only glimpses of his future, in omens, portents, and prophecies (as is only to be expected of a Roman hero) and (as is all-important for a questing hero) in sleep and dreams.

His first attempts to settle his Trojan followers, in Thrace and in Crete, have been calamitous failures. The Italy to which his ancestral gods have thereafter directed him has proved to be a promised land ever receding, as impossible to grasp as the scattered leaves that, disturbed from their 'thistledowny sequence'[10] in the Sibyl's cave, drift upwards whenever a draft of air is admitted. Aeneas, like all heroes, must learn through suffering, and so he has not been told of all the labours that await him in his new land, just as he does not yet know that he will found a race that will rule the world as long as time will last. But it will all come true. *Sic volvere Parcas.* So the Fates volve the scroll.

But even as *fatum*, the spoken decree of Jupiter, propels the hero onwards, *furor*, the irrational force embodied in Juno, constantly opposes him. That is Virgil's dialectical scheme of things. *Fatum*, the creative force in the cosmos and in human events, is forever opposed, in the cosmos and in human hearts, by *furor*. Virgil's hero is not Homer's self-reliant and resourceful survivor. He is a lonely figure caught up in history's swirl, the human agent of a more than human purpose, chosen by *fatum* to achieve its evolutionary purposes in history, and responding to his heroic role out of a sense of duty, or *pietas*.

So it is that, in the first five books of the poem, Juno's *furor* has, in a last attempt to keep Aeneas from Italy, blown him off his course, and he has been detained for a disastrous year by Queen Dido in Carthage, loving and, in obedience to *fatum* and his own sense of *pietas*, leaving her. She, in the end an instrument of Juno's flaming *furor*, has slain herself, cursing his memory. Other sacrificial deaths have been demanded of him – the death of his father in Sicily and, as an offering demanded by the god of the sea for his safe passage to Italy, the death of his trusty helmsman, Palinurus, at the cape not far from Cumae still called Capo di Palinuro.

Though I find myself moved, as many through the centuries

have been, by the deaths of Dido and of the hero's father, it is the death of Palinurus at the end of Book 5 that is, to me, the most beautiful thing Virgil ever wrote, suffused as it is with Virgilian doubts about the goodness of God and with Virgilian sadness at the realization that, for anything to be accomplished in this world, the innocent must suffer and die: Venus has pleaded with Neptune that her son Aeneas and his Trojans be allowed to reach Italy at last, and Neptune has demanded in return one sacrificial death. The passage has its share of gently ironic Virgilian subtleties: when the god of sleep bids the helmsman *pone caput*, the phrase can mean both 'Lay down your head' and 'Lay down your life.' Then the helmsman's eyes are quietly set aswim before the helmsman himself is cast into the pitiless deep. The passage is also one of those touching places in the narrative in which the poet addresses one of his characters:

And now dewy night had almost reached the midpoint of heaven. The sailors were sprawled on their rough benches by the oars below deck, their limbs softened and still. And the god Sleep came lightly gliding down from the stars of heaven, parted the airy darkness, and pushed the shadows aside. He was looking for you, Palinurus, bringing you harmful dreams, innocent one.

The god took his place on the high stern, in the likeness of [the mate] Phorbas, and poured out these words from his lips: 'Palinurus, son of Iasus, the sea itself is carrying the fleet on its way. The wind is steady. It is the hour for rest. Lay down your head. Steal your weary eyes away from your labours. I will take your place for a little while.'

And Palinurus, hardly lifting his eyes, said to him, 'Do you think I cannot see what lies beyond this calm surface, these peaceful waves? Do you want me to put my faith in the devil sea, to entrust Aeneas to treacherous winds – I, who have been deceived so often by the lure of a clear sky?'

He spoke and, holding fast to the tiller, never let loose his grasp, and kept his eyes fixed on the stars. But look! The god is passing around his head a branch dripping with the dew of Lethe, steeped in Stygian power.

And then, though the helmsman hesitated, the god lulled his swimming eyes. Scarcely had slumber made his limbs grow slack when the god, hovering over him, cast him headlong into the transparent waters, and as he fell he tore away the helm, and even a part of the stern, and called, many times and in vain, for his comrades.

Then the god lifted himself on his wings into thin air ... And when father Aeneas felt his ship drifting aimless, without its helmsman, he guided the craft himself through the waters of night, shaken to his soul over the fate of his friend. 'Oh, Palinurus,' he wept, 'you trusted too much in a calm sea and sky. And now you shall lie naked on an unknown shore.' (5.835–71)

That is the last passage we read before we volve the scroll to Virgil's great book, Book 6, with its Cumaean descent to 'that deep dark place in the self where the roots of the self begin.' Aeneas, as so often, is kept in the dark as to what has really happened. Characteristically, he weeps over the fate that has befallen someone who was as a son to him,[11] but, dutiful as always, he does not question the wisdom of it.

So, at the start of Book 6, Aeneas's ships put in at last at Cumae, and the hero, with his faithful aide-de-camp Achates, begins his Roman quest. He proceeds upwards from the shore through the dark grove of the goddess Diana to the temple precinct of Diana's brother, the prophetic Apollo – through the darkness of the moon upwards to the light of the sun. Arrived on the cliff of Cumae, Aeneas stares in wonder at the temple's gold-blazoned doors that, strangely, depict his past in terms of the myths of others. He is like the Theseus he sees on the golden doors: Theseus abandoned Ariadne, and he, *pius Aeneas*, has abandoned Dido. He is like the Daedalus he sees on the golden doors: Daedalus lost a son to the sea and he, *pater Aeneas*, has lost to the sea the innocent Palinurus.

The foundations of the Apollo temple that once represented those scenes, and the ruins of another, higher temple dedicated to Jupiter, still overlook the sea from Cumae's rock. The golden doors engraved by Daedalus are long since gone, but Virgil's hexameters about the graving of those doors are themselves engraved on a plaque nearby. Over the centuries the temples have served Greeks (they overlooked the famous naval battle in 474 BC when Hieron of Syracuse led his Greek Italians against the Etruscans and Carthaginians), then Romans (Augustus restored them about the time Virgil was writing), and, eventually, Christians. Now time has taken its toll again.

As I stood there, the graven lines of Virgil, the ruined temples, the volcanic cliff, the sea, the wind, and the sky all conspired together. I was glad that I had come to the site alone.

Suddenly, as Aeneas muses over the golden figures, the Sibyl of Cumae is there on the height, brusque and mannish, brought by faithful Achates. 'This is no time to gaze at pictures,' she says abruptly, without introduction. The past is done. Aeneas's future awaits him. He has come here to consult her. He should descend with her now to her cave.

Alone on the height, I got my own brusque reminder to descend. The wind picked up. Seawards a storm was on its way. I descended, with no faithful Achates to companion me, to the Sibyl's cave. It was dark within. Overhead the storm broke. The temperature dropped suddenly. Lightning cracked. Flashes glanced through the lateral fenestrations. Then the rains came.

In Book 6, the Sibyl tells Aeneas in this very cave that his past will repeat itself, that the old struggles will return, that terrible forces will continue to oppose him. But he must not despair. He must press on all the more bravely. His mission is civilizing. He must found Rome. He must father a new race.

What Aeneas says to that is 'Let me see my father. Show me the way to him.' His dead father has appeared to him in a dream and asked him to come to him in the world of the dead. And the entrance to that world is there, at Cumae.

The Sibyl answers that, if he wants to undertake this quest, he has to find and pluck a special talisman. Perhaps we are not surprised, after reading how Palinurus went to his death, to hear that the talisman is a bough:

'It lurks here on a dark tree, a bough of pliant golden leaves and stem, consecrated to Juno of the lower world. All the forest, all the valleys round conspire to hide it in darkness. But only he can pass beneath the hidden places of earth who has plucked from its tree the golden-haired spray. The beautiful goddess below has so decreed: it must be brought to her, as her proper offering. And when the bough is broken away, a second appears – golden too, for the branch will always blossom with the selfsame metal. Search it out, then. Lift up your eyes. Find it. Take it in your hand. If fate is calling you, the bough will follow your hand willingly and with ease. If not, no strength, no sword will avail you to win it or sunder it.' (6.136–48)

The Golden Bough, the Holy Grail, the sword in the stone, the blue flower, the blue bird – whatever the talisman or mystic goal, the hero, the knight, the future king, the wondering child has to find it. It is, or at least it has been since Virgil, the emblem of the quest.

Overhead, the rain stopped as quickly as it had come. I climbed to ground level and – pedestrian thought! – took the wet path forward in hope eventually of finding, not a golden bough, but a bus back to civilization. The wind had fallen. I walked for an hour between the sea and the sky, perhaps along the path once walked by Aeneas and the faithful Achates. The Sibyl had told them of yet another victim demanded for the onward progress of the hero on his mission: they would find a body unburied, polluting the shore. We think, as we read, that the body washed naked to shore will be that of Palinurus. But on the sand they find, washed ashore, not the body of Aeneas's helmsman but that of his trumpeter, Misenus.

As I walked, a rainbow began to form ahead, and beneath it stood a small figure. A barefoot boy. He seemed to have appeared out of nowhere on the landscape. 'Si, signore, si,' he answered my questions. 'There is a bus. I saw it waiting for you. At Licola. You go this way, please.'

And at Licola, mirabile dictu, there was a local bus, strangely empty, bound for Pozzuoli. I knew that from there I could get a train back to Naples.

I was not, then, called by fate to find and pluck the Golden Bough that blossomed somewhere in the forests of this volcanic landscape. Instead I was sent, as by an apparition, back to my ordinary life and my teaching, that year, of the Classics in Rome. It appeared that I was not, from circumstances, to see Lake Avernus, which was Virgil's entrance to the underworld.

But the bus left the sea and veered unexpectedly back into Virgil country, and suddenly from my window I looked down on Averno, peacefully filling its volcanic crater. In Virgil's day, Agrippa, in need of a naval base, had had a canal dug to connect Lake Avernus to nearby Lake Lucrinus and to the sea. But now, as in the legendary time of Aeneas, the lake is land-locked again, fed by springs from below. Its surface that day was pure and still and glistening in the afternoon sun. There was no sign of the hellish cave Virgil put within the crater's rim, exhaling mephitic fumes deadly to any birds that flew overhead. But the lake was still surrounded by trees sufficently to conjure up images of the vaster forest where, led by two doves sent by his mother Venus, Aeneas found his Golden Bough. And in the distance there still loomed the misty, flat-topped eminence where the trumpeter Misenus received his burial rites. (It is called Monte Miseno to this day.) Aeneas was with his Trojans, felling trees to make the funeral pyre of his trumpeter when, as Virgil says:

A pair of doves came gliding down from the sky before his eyes and lighted on the green grass. The great hero knew at once that these birds were his mother's, and he joyfully prayed, 'Lead me on, if there be any way! From high above direct my course to the grove where the precious bough casts its shadow on the fruitful earth. And you, my goddess mother, fail me not in this my hour of need!' He spoke, and stopped in his tracks to see what signal the doves would give, which way they would fly. And they flew on, and fed, and flew on again, just so far at any time as any follower could keep them in his ken. And when they came to the jaws of sulfurous Avernus, they flew upwards, swiftly, where the air was clear, and came down to rest on a tree of two natures: there shone out through the branches a gleam not like the colour of the rest – a gleam of gold. (6.190–204)

Here is where Virgil introduces one of his most sensuous comparisons:

Just as in the cold of winter the mistletoe will bloom in the forest with fresh leaves – while the tree on which it appears has not engendered it – and just as the mistletoe wreathes the shapely tree with yellow growth, such was the sight of the blazing gold on the shadowy oak, and such the sound when the metal jangled in the gentle wind. (6.205–9)

In the Latin hexameter that last line is a fine example of Virgil's magical way with sounds. The line jangles quietly at first and then, as the texture changes from thin *i*- and light *l*- to heavy *b*-, percussive *t*-, and broad *a*- sounds, it flutters open in the wind:

> ilice sic leni crepitabat brattea vento.

And Virgil continues:

Aeneas plucked the bough instantly. It hesitated – but the hero broke it away eagerly, and carried it to the Sibyl's cave. (6.210–11)

With the Golden Bough, found after the sacrificial death of the trumpeter Misenus, Aeneas is ready to begin the quest that lies within his larger mission to found Rome – the journey directed by his mother to his father. The archetypal quest to prove him a hero to himself.

No talisman carried on any quest has more mystery about it than Virgil's Golden Bough. Commentators since the first-century Cornutus seem agreed that it is Virgil's own invention, a fiction[12] of his own imagination, but nonetheless fashioned by him from various sources. There are at least four problems with it that no one – not even Eduard Norden or Jackson Knight or R.A. Brooks or (in a pioneering two-part article) Charles Segal or (in a deliciously cranky article) David West – has solved completely. Why is Aeneas's talisman a bough? Why is it golden? Why is it compared to mistletoe? And, most tantalizingly, why –when the hero is told it will come willingly or not at all – does it come neither way? Why, in Virgil's tantalizing word *cunctantem*, does it hesitate?

Virgil's bough calls first to my Homeric mind the plant *mōly* given by Hermes to Odysseus to protect him from the malevolent Circe, who is rendered harmless by it and, like the Sibyl in Virgil, tells the hero how to reach the lands of the dead.[13]

To other minds Virgil's Golden Bough will suggest immediately the bough that provided the title for Sir James George Frazer's vast compendium of comparative mythologies. Frazer actually found the starting point for his *magnum opus* in the commentary on Book 6 of Virgil written by the fourth-century grammarian Servius. But the bough Servius, and then Frazer, spoke of is much older than Virgil. It had to be plucked not at Cumae near Naples but at the grove of Lake Nemi in the Alban Hills near Rome, and by whatever runaway slave sought to challenge in mortal combat the priest of the local cult of Diana. If successful, the slave would rule the cult himself – until he was slain in turn by the next runaway slave who plucked a bough and issued the challenge.[14] Virgil, with his interest in myth and ritual, would likely have known something of this strange tradition: he is careful to introduce a grove to Diana at his Cumae and to make his bough, like the bough at Nemi, a certification of the bearer's qualifications.

But Virgil's bough qualifies the bearer, not for a priesthood, but for a journey through the underworld. I rather think it owes more to the bough-like staff carried by Mercury when he escorts human souls to their places in the world of the dead. Horace mentions that shuddery bough, that *virga horrida*, in a famous ode (1.24) addressed to Virgil. That *virga* is possibly one of the reasons the spelling of Virgil's name was changed, in later ages, from 'Vergil' to 'Virgil.' In any case, it is a symbol of passage from life to life-after-death. And that, I think, is why Virgil, remembering his own 'death of Palinurus,' made his hero's talisman a bough.[15]

Why is the bough Aeneas must pluck golden? For the perfectly good reason, most commentators say, that gold is the metal most suited, by its preciousness, for a quest: the other famous object of a heroic journey in classical myth is a Golden Fleece, and one of Heracles's twelve labours was to pluck the golden apples of the Hesperides. More important, gold was the colour of Mercury's shuddery bough: Horace calls it an *aurea virga* in *Odes* 1.10. Gold is, as Segal notes, following Norden, 'traditionally connected in antiquity with the dead' and 'associated with immortality.'[16]

Others will connect Virgil's bough with one referred to by the

Greek lyric poet Meleager who, writing slightly before Virgil, had spoken of 'the golden bough of the ever-divine Plato, gleaming everywhere in goodness.'[17] As the revelation Virgil will give his hero in the underworld owes something to the myth of Er in the last book of Plato's *Republic*, it is possible, and attractive, to think that Virgil might have made his hero's bough golden as a luminous tribute to his myth-making predecessor.

But I'd like to advance, in place of all of these, an association via Jung from a book on Wagner: gold, in myth and in dreams, 'is traditionally associated with the light of the sun and thus with consciousness, just as silver is associated with the moon and with that indirect illumination which is somehow reflected back from the unconscious.'[18] Commentators on Book 6 of the *Aeneid* note, often without thinking it worthy of explication, that the Golden Bough is necessary for Aeneas only on what they have called the first half of his journey beneath the earth. Aeneas leaves the bough at the gateway that leads from one half of the underworld to the other. What is not sufficiently noted by commentators is that the first half of the journey underground is a passage through a realm lit as if by the light of a deceitful moon, and that the second half, beyond the arched gateway, is a radiant land with its own sky, lit by its own sun. The Golden Bough is not needed there; it is needed only for passage through the moon-lit land where Aeneas and the Sibyl go *obscuri sola sub nocte per umbram*:

dark under the lonely night through the shadows ... as when by a fitful moon, under its malignant light, there is a path in the forest, when God has hid the sky in darkness, and black night has taken the colour out of everything. (6.268–72)

Aeneas, I venture to say, needs the Golden Bough's sunlike gleam of consciousness only as he makes his way through the moonlit and often illusory part of his unconscious. The underworld journey of Aeneas may, then, be thought a journey through the two parts of his own unconscious: the darkness and the light of it, the moon and the sun of it, the feminine and the masculine of it, the part given access to by his mother and the part that leads to his father. I shall come back eventually to those thoughts prompted by the gold of the bough.

Why is the bough compared to mistletoe? Why does Virgil, by pictorial and onomatopoeic effects, suggest that it looked like the mistletoe's yellow flowers, and even sounded like mistletoe rustling in the wind? Brooks is helpful here: the mistletoe seems in the depth of winter to be alive when all else in the forest appears dead; yet paradoxically the forest trees are really alive, and it is the mistletoe that is dead. Mistletoe, a parasite, has no life of its own. It draws its sustenance from the apparently dead tree that supports it. As a kind of reverse-image of life-amid-death, the mistletoe effectively symbolizes the experience of the hero who will pass living through a dead world.[19]

Frazer devotes a large part of his vast work to the mistletoe, which was thought, especially among the Druids, the 'oak-knowing' priests of Celtic Europe, to have magic properties.[20] Virgil may well have known something of the ceremonies and beliefs of the Druids. (Julius Caesar and the elder Pliny certainly did, and no less a Virgilian than Eduard Norden saw a Celtic significance in Virgil's mistletoe-simile.[21]) There is in Druid ritual a link between the moon, ritual purity, the oak tree, and the cutting of the mistletoe – all of them brought together, for this opera-goer, in the entrance of the Druid priestess Norma in Bellini's opera of that name: a trumpet sounds a march, and Norma enters to cut the mistletoe from its oak and sing her 'Casta Diva' to the chaste moon. If the Druids, like the Old Testament Jews, sounded a trumpet[22] at the new moon, we have a ritual to match every detail of Virgil's sequence: Aeneas is preparing the purificatory funeral of his trumpeter when he discovers the oak in the forest; he plucks the mistletoe-like talisman and descends with it to the moonlit part of the land below. We can make no definitive statements here. All we can say is that mistletoe had in abundance the mysterious associations that Virgil wanted for his Golden Bough.

Why, finally, does the bough hesitate? This is, for any discussion of the quest, the most important question. Servius was only the first to feel that he had somehow to explain away Virgil's tantalizing participle *cunctantem* (hesitating): he said, unconvincingly, that Virgil had the bough hesitate simply to show by contrast how eager Aeneas was to pluck it.[23] The late Virgilian editor Deryck Williams, with whom I have respectfully disagreed in public more than once, has also tried to explain *cunctantem* away: Virgil's participle 'refers quite appropriately to the natural resistance of a plant with pliant stem to being picked off'.[24] The Oxford editor Sir Frank Fletcher observes along the same lines that *cunctantem* is simply 'used adjectivally in the sense of "sluggish,"' that it is similarly 'applied to soil by Virgil and to honey by Lucretius.'[25] These Virgilians seem to forget that Virgil has the Sibyl say quite specifically that the Golden Bough is *metallic* both in leaves and stem (6.137). It has nothing of a natural plant or of soil or of honey about it. R.G. Austin, in his more complete commentary, chooses to dismiss the whole matter as quickly as he can.[26]

I cannot. It seems to me that something more than sluggish and natural resistance is implied in *cunctantem*, when the bough that Aeneas was told would come *volens facilisque* – willingly and readily, or else not at all – does neither, but hesitates. *Volens* is, I think, the operative word not given sufficient attention by Virgil's editors.[27] Talismans in quest legends *will* of their own accord who is to find them. The Holy Grail itself determines who is worthy to find it. This is fundamental to the whole notion of a religious vocation ('You have not chosen me, I have chosen you'), and indeed of any true vocation. One has to be called to it. The Sibyl tells Aeneas that the bough will follow his hand *volens*, of its *own* will, if *fatum* is calling him. Yet the bough hesitates.

Cunctantem, hesitating, is, I have often thought, one of those lonely Virgilian words wherein Tennyson sees 'all the charm of all the Muses flowering.' It recurs thoughout the *Aeneid* thematically, like a Wagnerian leitmotif.[28] Virgil uses it, always in the oblique cases of its participial form, for moments when his characters are faced with decisions that will influence all their lives, and sometimes even end their lives. He reserves *cunctantem* for the great, pivotal moments in his epic. Dido, before she departs on the royal hunt that will change her life, lingers in her tent: *cunctantem* (4.133). Aeneas, watching Dido succumb to madness, cannot bring himself to speak the words he wants to say: *cunctantem* (4.390). Palinurus, lulled to sleep by a Lethean bough, tries, before he falls sacrificially to his death in the sea, to resist: *cunctanti* (5.856). The Italian hero Turnus, when we first meet him threatened with *furor* by a winged fury, resists: *cunctantem* (7.449). Turnus again, at the moment of truth, faced with a final winged fury, wavers: *cunctantem* (12.919). On the poem's last page, Aeneas himself, poised to kill Turnus, is momentarily deflected by his opponent's prayers from making the final thrust: *cunctantem* (12.940). And the bough that was to qualify Aeneas for his hero's mission freely or not at all, for just a moment, hesitates: *cunctantem* (6.211).

Virgil even depicts the creative artist's climactic moment, when he must surrender to inspiration, in these terms: Vulcan, for just a moment, resists the embrace of Venus that will send the lightning flash through his frame and empower him, after sleep, to create the figures on the hero's shield: *cunctantem* (8.388).

Every single instance of the participle is weighted with these intimations of the fated moment and of human, even divine, resistance to it. The Golden Bough hesitates, it seems to me, because at that point in Book 6 a great moment is at hand. The bough wonders – for Virgil's *volens* grants it sentience – if Aeneas is truly qualified, divinely destined, for his mission. 'Si te fata vocant,' says the Sibyl. 'If fate is calling you.' *Fatum* is the force that sweeps the *Aeneid* onward. But when the moment of vocation comes for *pius Aeneas*, the sign of *fatum* itself hesitates, for a moment, to call him.

Aeneas does of course pluck the bough and make his journey, with the Sibyl at his side holding the bough under her cloak, through the moonlit underworld. He leaves the bough at the threshold leading to the sunlit place where, deep in a green valley, he meets his father:

And when the father saw Aeneas coming to him across the grass, he stretched forth both his hands in happiness, and tears streamed down his cheeks, and a cry fell from his lips: 'Have you come at last? Has the *pietas* in which your father placed his hope seen you through this perilous journey? Can it be that I see your face, my son, and hear your voice again, and speak with you? Oh, I knew it in my heart. I was sure, as I counted the days, that this time would come, and my longing has not failed me. I have you here, my son, after you have crossed so many lands and seas, and passed by so many perils!' (6.684–94)

We cannot help thinking here of the scene between Odysseus and his father, though Virgil, with his customary denseness of allusion, has based his passage equally on the meeting, in a waking dream, of Achilles and the ghost of his friend Patroclus in *Iliad* 23, and he has virtually quoted the opening line of Catullus's famous poem 101, where the poet, after a long journey, comes to the tomb of his brother. The love of father, friend, and brother all radiate from Virgil's lines.

In that secluded vale (*in valle reducta*) where Aeneas finds his father, he receives from him something of an answer to the mysteries of life and death. The answer – part Plato, part Pythagoras, part Orphic, part Stoic, and, in its language, part Epicurean – begins with a description of 'universal Nature ruled by universal Mind' and of human souls redeeming themselves through a series of reincarnations, and it climaxes in a forecast of the long Roman future Aeneas will initiate. As the Romans who will conquer the world and then turn upon themselves in civil war pass before the hero's eyes, there is a suggestion, with the father's excursus on metempsychosis, that after the passage of a thousand years his son will be reincarnated as founding Romulus, and then, after the passage of a thousand more, as saving Augustus. Above all, the father tells his son, he must remember that his mission as a Roman will be

to rule the world with empire, to impose a law of peace, to spare the submissive but to make utter war on the rebellious. (6.850–2)

The first words of the *Aeneid* are *arma virumque* – arms and the man. Here at the heart of the poem, we are assured that the arms this man will use will be arms used in the interest of world peace.

But in the last lines of Book 6, as the father speeds his son back to the world above, there are doubts about all of this. We come now to another celebrated and still unresolved Virgilian problem. My own exit from the Cumae area was, after an initial difficulty, expedited by a conveyence unpromised and unexpected, and the whole experience has lived in my memory vividly. Aeneas's exit is very problematic, and he seems thereafter to remember his Cumaean experience dimly, if at all. The Sibyl told him that his descent to the underworld would be easy (*facilis descensus Averno*) but his return journey difficult (*hoc opus, hic labor est*), and indeed the questions we asked about the Golden Bough needed for the entrance to the underworld are easy to answer compared to the questions we must now raise about the exit therefrom. In fact, the last lines of Book 6 are the most baffling of all the passages in Virgil. *Sunt gemini Somni portae*, Virgil says:

There are twin gates of Sleep. One is said to be of horn, and thereby an easy exit is given to true shades. The other, glistening and crafted of gleaming ivory, is the gate whereby the spirits send up false dreams to the world above. (6.893–6)

And Virgil continues: 'The father, done with his prophecies, escorted his son and the Sibyl to, and sent them forth by, the ivory gate.' The reader usually notes only after he has read on a few lines to the end of the book that the ivory gate through which Aeneas has exited is the gate, not of true, but of false dreams.

What can Virgil have meant?

Not, as Norden suggested, simply that Aeneas and the Sibyl exited before midnight, according to a Roman superstition that only dreams dreamed after midnight came true.[29] The Sibyl does, in the journey through the underworld, remind Aeneas when it is noon in the world above, and thereafter hurries him onwards; but, as Wendell Clausen says, 'I have a sense ... that Virgil was not merely telling the time of night.'[30]

What then *was* he saying? The two gates were well known in literature before Virgil. Penelope, as we observed in our previous chapter, mentions them in the *Odyssey*: some dreams come true, she tells Odysseus, others do not. She makes little puns in Greek on horn (*keras*) and fulfil (*krainō*), and on ivory (*elephas*) and deceive (*elephairomai*).[31] Similarly, there may be some significance in Virgil's Latin words for horn (*cornea*) and ivory (*elephanto*): the gates in Latin may be gates of eye and tooth, of what passes through the eye and what escapes the Homeric 'barrier of the teeth,' of things *seen* to be true and things only *said* to be true. So Fletcher suggests that Virgil's intent was to tell us that the book's contents are 'not what his own eyes have seen, but what he has heard from others'[32] – presumably from initiates of Orphic or other mysteries about reincarnation.

That is an attractive suggestion. Much of what father Anchises tells Aeneas, before he speeds him out of the ivory gate, *is* about reincarnation. The principal doctrine of the Druids, Julius Caesar tells us, is that the soul is immortal and passes at death to another body. And Virgil's Latin, we note on closer inspection, changes Homer's Greek: Virgil's gate of horn sends forth, not dreams, but souls to be reincarnated. Austin says that that is why the hero and the Sibyl have to exit through the other gate – they are not souls leaving the underworld for a new existence.[33]

But to have that other gate a false gate – can Virgil have intended *that*, after the glorious future his hero has been promised?

Yes, thinks Servius (we're back with him in these labyrinthine wanderings): Virgil, he says, obviously wants it understood that everything he has said in the book is false: *et poetice apertus est sensus: vult enim intelligi falsa esse omnia quae dixit.*[34] Some modern critics have actually followed Servius in that astonishing statement, though they moderate it somewhat. Virgil, they say, is expressing his dissatisfaction with the religious, philosophical, and historical views expressed in Book 6. Well, I think that Edward Gibbon rather neatly scotched those suggestions: 'I had much rather reproach my favourite author with want of care in one line than with want of taste throughout a whole book.'[35]

What, then, shall *I* say?

I shall come back to the most powerful man in the world – Octavian, soon to be named Augustus. I shall say that, when Virgil was invited by Octavian, perhaps at the intervention of his cultural attaché Maecenas, to write an epic in praise of his *res gestae*, the poet understandably hesitated. He had doubts, first, about himself. He was only a miniaturist, a Roman Alexandrian, writing in the smaller genres earlier Roman Alexandrians like Catullus had not yet attempted – the pastoral and the didactic poem. And, if Ronald Syme is right about Octavian,[36] Virgil might have had doubts as well about that opportunistic young man who had become, after the battle of Actium, so very powerful. Would this man who had waded through so much blood to become, as he was increasingly called, *pater patriae* and Augustus – would he give the world peace after a century of war? Or would every Roman's worst fears be realized?

Virgil, wisely, wrote the epic asked of him. Other poets – Gallus and Ovid – who did not please Augustus came to bad ends. Virgil wrote his epic, but it was not an epic written simply to please a man in power. It is not, as it is sometimes said to be, merely a piece of propaganda. It traces Augustus's career, not in a versified chronicle of glorified campaigns and victories, but in a Latin *Odyssey* and *Iliad*[37] in which Augustus is made into a fallible and imperfect Aeneas – chosen by fate to lead his people from the ashes of a fallen city through countless struggles to a new land, from republic to empire. But, Virgil wonders at the great moments in the poem, will the new foundation bring peace? Will it be worth the cost in human lives? Will it be worth the sufferings of the innocent?

Those are questions that hang over all three of Virgil's works. Will this powerful man be the young god who, at the start of the *Eclogues*, gives peace, or will he prove to be the brutal soldier there who evicts the peaceful from their homes? Will this powerful man be the young god Aristaeus who, at the close of the *Georgics*, acknowledges his past destructiveness and only then succeeds in restoring the civilized society – the bees – he has nurtured? Is this now all-powerful man, at the mid-point of the *Aeneid*, really called by fate to accomplish the mission of rebuilding Rome? The Sibyl tells him, not without some doubt, that he will pluck the Golden Bough '*si te fata vocant.*' But the Golden Bough hesitates. And even after the hero has seen a vision of the Roman future, Virgil's doubts crowd in:

sed falsa ad caelum mittunt insomnia manes

but the spirits send false dreams, too, to the upper world.

The Virgilian dream that Augustus's soul once animated the body, some thousand years before, of founding Romulus and, some thousand years before that, of father Aeneas, is not a dream in which the poet, even while suggesting the possibility, has complete confidence. His *Aeneid* does not end with reconciliation, peace, and the establishment of a new civilization. After the journey through the underworld in Book 6, the epic presses on with wars in which Aeneas often offends against the *pietas* that makes him a hero. Several events in his wars strikingly parallel terrible incidents reported of Augustus when he was still Octavian, during Rome's civil wars. In Book 10, in revenge for the slaying of a surrogate son he has promised to protect, Aeneas takes eight young sons from among the enemy as captives to be slaughtered at the boy's funeral, and then proceeds to slay a succession of unfortunates who appeal to him in the name of *pietas*, in the name of their fathers. As he slays, Aeneas speaks words close to those reported of Octavian when he avenged the death of his adoptive father, Julius Caesar.[38] Virgil's doubts about Octavian/Augustus increase with each turn of the scroll, and his poem finally leaves the reader hanging, hesitating, *cunctantem* – as Aeneas slays, at the scroll's end, the enemy who pleads with him for his life in the name of both their fathers.

In short, I think that Augustus, the primary reader of the poem that depicts his career in mythic terms, is, on that last page, shown *himself* at a moment in history – in 19 BC, with his enemies dead but his mission still unfulfilled. He still has not proved that he was the one called to give Rome a new birth. The dream of the future has not yet come true. The Golden Bough was right to hesitate.

This, it need hardly be said, is not Homer. This hero's quest is not completed. This author, 'majestic in [his] sadness at the doubtful doom of humankind,' remains ambivalent to the end: *cunctantem*. That is the way most of us on this side of the Atlantic have read the *Aeneid* in recent years.[39] It is a melancholy assessment. The poem is not a eulogy in praise of empire but a meditation on it that finds it wanting. It is a quest that, at the moment of writing, had yet to find completion.

How has all of this affected our ongoing definition of the quest? I cannot leave the Virgilian landscape we have surveyed from this labryrinthine bus ride without adding some details from Virgil that redefine the observations we made in Homer.

Virgil's hero, like Homer's, faces his archetypes. And first among them, still rather tentatively depicted but clearer than in Homer, is the preliminary figure in Jung's pattern – the shadow. The companions of questing heroes invariably complement them with utterly different, often compensatory, qualities. So the kingly Gilgamesh was companioned by the animalistic Enkidu. So, in works closer to our time, the high-minded Prince Tamino makes his journey in company with that unsophisticated child of nature, the bird-man Papageno. The lean, visionary idealist, Don Quixote, is accompanied by that plump and consummate realist, Sancho Panza. Even the astute Sherlock Holmes has as his companion an often uncomprehending Dr Watson, needed mostly to do the footwork and, eventually, to record the adventures. Often with the companion figure there is a colour difference. Huck Finn sails down the Mississippi with black Jim and (in the popular myths of my boyhood) the Lone Ranger rides with what radio then called a redskin, Tonto, and the Green Hornet with a Japanese (but, during the Second World War, a friendly Philippino) valet, Kato.

Aeneas has as his companion Achates, whom Williams, wiser perhaps than he knows, calls 'a very colorless figure.'[40] Jung, tracing the archetype in the dreams of his patients, says that the shadow represents the inward qualities of the hero that are not part of the outer persona, that part of the hero which remains unseen but nonetheless attached: Achates, we note, shelters unseen with Aeneas in a cloud.

The shadow can, if unbefriended, oppose the hero and attempt to destroy him, as the dwarf Mime does Wagner's heroic Siegfried, and as – in a single figure – the evil Mr Hyde opposes and destroys the good Dr Jekyll. But if the hero acknowledges and befriends his shadow, he 'greatly enhances his potential for psychic growth and, as the shadow is in contact with his unconscious, is strengthened in his conscious pursuits.'[41]

So it is that Achates is the only one of his men in whom Aeneas confides. (Allegorical interpretations[42] of the *Aeneid* sometimes identify him as one or the other of Augustus's two close friends, as Agrippa or Maecenas.) Achates knows the hero at a deeper level: he alone hears Aeneas speak his famous line about the *lacrimae rerum*, the world's tears. Achates is not only perceptive – the first in North Africa to strike the spark from flint and light the fire and the first to sight Italy from the sea – but, more than most of the shadow-figures we have noted, he has a connection, as a Jungian shadow should, with the hero's feminine side. At Carthage he is alone with the hero when he encounters his mother Venus. The four lines (1.582–5) that are his only words in the whole epic are about Aeneas's mother; they begin '*nate dea*' and end '*cetera matris.*' At Cumae he brings the Sibyl into Aeneas's presence. He is with Aeneas, on the site where Rome shall be built, when the hero's mother brings him his shield. He is at Aeneas's side when the hero is wounded and his mother appears again to remove the arrow from the wound. But he disappears for whole books when the hero is in no need of this connection with his feminine side.

The second of the archetypes the hero encounters, on subconscious as well as conscious levels, is Jung's ambivalent anima. Aeneas's onward journey, willed by father Jupiter, is constantly in danger from the interventions of maternal Juno. His *conscious* encounter with the feminine is, of course, with Dido – an encounter arranged, with the collusion of Juno, by his mother Venus, who appears to him dressed as Diana, the moon goddess to whom Dido will be compared. His *unconscious* encounter with the feminine comes in the moonlit part of the underworld, in a landscape lit as if by the *luce maligna* of an untrustworthy moon (*per incertam lunam*). There Aeneas meets in succession three apparitions – the ghosts of Palinurus, Dido, and Helen's husband Deiphobus – that may easily be construed as manifestations of the Jungian anima: what they say is remarkably inconsistent with what we have been told of the experiences of Palinurus, Dido, and Helen among the living. The anima, as Jung discovered in his clinical work, attempts to arrest the patient under treatment with pathetic visions that do not speak the truth. The Sibyl, like a good therapist, realizes the danger, answers the visions, and keeps hurrying the hero onwards.

The anima, a congeries of the hero's experience of the feminine, and of his fear of the feminine, must be encountered, its dangerous potential overcome, and its creative potential released, if the hero is ever to relate maturely to women in his conscious life. Aeneas failed with Dido. Will he succeed, with Lavinia, in founding a civilization? Virgil never tells us that. Many of the intimations are doubtful. But the hero does, with the Sibyl and the Golden Bough, successfully proceed through his feminine unconscious to the portal of Persephone. He does pass beyond the moonlit anima to the next archetype. In the sunlit part of the underworld, where even the feminine Sibyl must wonder and ask questions, the hero finally finds his father.

In this encounter with the Wise Old Man, Virgil gives us, at the heart of the poem, answers to the great questions he asked on his first page: 'Why do the innocent suffer?' and 'What is God?' The innocent suffer, we hear from the hero's father, as part of a cosmic process of purification in which individual souls pass through several existences. And God, we hear, is the cosmic force, the *deus*, *spiritus*, and *mens* directing the process.

These are partial answers at best. I have the feeling that Virgil, who at his death left them in strangely unpoetic hexameters, didn't think them the last word on his great questions. The ambivalence of the two gates confounds us with the next turn of the scroll. And just before that we are given a glimpse of a future in which a tragic limit is put to Rome's greatness: father Anchises exclaims 'heu, miserande puer' as he tells his son that Rome, at its proudest moment, will lose its fondest hope. Augustus's chosen successor, his adoptive son Marcellus, will die:

'Alas, pitiable boy! If only in some way you could burst the stern bonds of *fatum*! You will be Marcellus. Give me lilies by the handful. Let me scatter shining flowers. Let me lavish them at least as gifts for the soul of my descendant. Let me perform for him that ceremony, though it cannot bring him back to life.' (6.882–6)[43]

Marcellus, a historical figure, lies at the centre of Virgil's mythic poem – the hope for the future, dead at age nineteen of undiscovered causes, emblemed in the deaths of Palinurus and Misenus we have already spoken of and, in the battle books that follow Book 6, in the young deaths of Euryalus and Nisus, of Pallas and Lausus.[44] Had Marcellus lived to fulfil all of Augustus's hopes, the whole known world might have been Romanized, and the history of Europe, and perhaps of much more than Europe, might have been different – from the severing of Roman West and Greek East in Byzantine times to the Renaissance in Romanized Europe that was a Reformation elsewhere to the two world wars fought largely across the Rhine by non-Latin against Latin cultures. What if Marcellus had lived to rule with empire all of the Western world, to pacify it and impose upon it a *pax Romana*? Would our histories have been the same? Virgil inevitably prompts such questions. He has been thought across the centuries to have foreseen the history of the West. He certainly saw in the death of Marcellus in his own day a sign that heaven had set a limit to Roman, and perhaps to human, achievement.

Does Virgil's hero complete his quest? That completion should be marked by a symbol of the self, integrated, inviolate, centripetal. Before he enters on his wars, Aeneas is given his circle with centripetal patterns, his mandala – the shield blazoned with golden depictions of the future of Rome, all of them centred around Augustus's great victory at Actium. Like the revelation of the future of Rome given the hero by his father *in valle reducta*, the wondrous shield is brought to the hero by his mother *in valle reducta*. Homer's Achilles had been given such a shield by his mother in the *Iliad*, blazoned with scenes of war and peace, of civilization passing through nature's seasons, all of it centred in the cosmos of sun, moon, and stars. And by the end of the *Iliad*, Homer's hero may be thought to have completed his journey from savage wrath to civilizing forgiveness. But Virgil has his hero lift his Augustan shield on his shoulder *ignarus*, not really knowing what the golden figures mean. It was daring of Virgil to use that lonely word *ignarus* at that moment. How many of these ambivalent touches could he make without offending his imperial reader, who was certainly intelligent enough to see how ambivalently they might be read?

So it is that, at the end of Virgil's last scroll, his hero is, like Augustus himself when Marcellus died, still on the larger quest. Aeneas is poised to kill his enemy Turnus. Turnus pleads for mercy in the name of his father, who is old, as Aeneas's father once was old, and in need of a son. Each of Homer's poems had ended with an acknowledgment by the hero of the importance of his father in the completion of his journey. That is not to be the case here. Aeneas's father had told him, as in a field of light he looked into the future,

parcere subiectis et debellare superbos,

to make utter war on the rebellious, yes, but to spare the submissive. Through all his battles Aeneas has never once adverted to anything he learned from his father in the world below consciousness. But now, as Turnus pleads submissively, Aeneas seems at last to remember something from his father's words, something from the underworld journey his Golden Bough had brought him to: *parcere subiectis* – 'spare those who are submissive.' Poised to kill, Aeneas hesitates (the participle is, of course, *cunctantem*). Then, as the poem hurries to its end, he sees another gleam of gold, a blazoned design on the belt Turnus is wearing. The Sibyl had warned him when he saw the golden temple doors at Cumae that gazing on images could delay his progress. These images set his eyes rolling. It is as if his mind gives way, even as Dido long before had lost her reason *volvens oculos*. Aeneas sees blazoned in gold the figures of fifty young men slain in their prime – engraved on the belt once worn by the young man he had sworn to protect, and now adorning the enemy who had slain that young man. It is a moment in which many of the poem's leitmotifs come together.[45] Aeneas, filled suddenly with *furor*, forgets his father's words. The golden images tell him, fifty times over, to kill. And the hero, claiming that his act is *pietas*, hesitating for only a moment, kills.

The epic ends on that shockingly abrupt note. Some think Virgil ought to have concluded his epic with a sign of hope, with all passion spent, with a Trojan-Italian peace, with the hero entering into his promised glory.[46] But the few indications we have suggest that, though the poem never received his finishing touches, Virgil intended it to end where it does.[47] He wanted to conclude his epic by asking the man who asked for the epic, 'Will you continue to pursue political vengeance? Or will you remember the words of your father,[48] and give us peace? I have marked this poem with my doubts, which are the doubts of all the forces, natural and supernatural, you have encountered. Will you, in spite of them all, complete your civilizing mission?'

To some, such considerations will seem extraneous to the purpose of epic. They do not know what Virgil has done for epic. He has extended its scope so that it encompasses the whole history of the world he knows. He has pondered that world and looked to its long future. During the Second World War, when the world that Augustus never succeeded in forging into a Roman unity seemed about to be torn apart irrevocably by the tribes who were never Romanized, T.S. Eliot called the *Aeneid* 'the classic of all Europe.'[49] And he was able to say this because Virgil, adapting and learning from the traditions of centuries past, had given twenty centuries of European civilization a mature statement of the Roman culture that had brought it into being. After the war it was a German meditation titled *Vergil, Vater des Abendlandes* that enabled Eliot to celebrate the prophetic power of Virgil's writing for all the lands of the West: the *Eclogues*, the *Georgics*, and the *Aeneid* saw into the future even though their author might, like the Sibyl at Cumae, have been 'uttering something which he [did] not wholly understand.'[50]

Similarly, I can remember the late A. Bartlett Giamatti – the president of Yale who was at once major-league baseball's incorruptible commissioner and a perceptive reader of Spenser and Ariosto – saying that there was much more to epic than simply length, that it had also to define a world, and to show the failures and the horrors as well as the glories of that world. 'Great epics,' he said, 'illuminate man's need and man's capacity to control the demonic and destructive forces within him and around him.' More than that, they 'contain and include all that went before ... all previous epic poems.' He was speaking of Renaissance epics that created new visions by 'implicating, involving, borrowing from, echoing, and alluding to the *Aeneid*,' even as the *Aeneid* had created a new vision out of older Greek and Roman poetry and especially out of Homer. Echoing and alluding to Homer's epics, Virgil gave us a new idea of what epic could be: an epic could, if the vision is vast enough, be nothing less than 'an analogue to human history,'[51] a reflection on a whole civilization, a new kind of quest.

We haven't by any means exhausted what Virgil has to say about the quest. Maybe everything I have said here is false. Servius might have said so. Donald Oakley Robson might have said so. But I think my former teacher of Virgil would have agreed that, with Virgil, we're always invited to read and wonder more, confident that, while there may be no sure answers, in the very asking of the questions some vision has been communicated to those who have read the poem as a poem with meaning for themselves. As James Joyce once said, 'Volve the Virgil page and view.'

The more we read the majestically doubting Virgil, the more open we are to that sense of a transcendent of which Virgil is, in the West, the chief prophet. With his studied ambivalences, with his levels on levels of suggestive meanings, Virgil is the grave and constant opponent of all positivism, empiricism, dogmatism, and systematization. With his volcanic nowhere, his Golden Bough, his ivory gate, and his premature deaths of Palinurus and Marcellus, he is the everlasting questioner who knows that whatever answers there may be – about the nature of God, about human suffering and the meaning of history – lie beyond any of our systems of thought. How many doors, how many corridors are there in the cavernous passage where the voice of the Sibyl comes bounding? Six only? Not when the flashes of light come laterally through the fenestrations. There are hundreds.

Virgil is, in the end, inexhaustible. What is his contribution to our definition of the quest? That the quest can be a paradigm for history. That human history can never be explained without a sympathetic understanding of the ambivalences of human nature. That no man is perfect, though those chosen by the gods to lead us may have in them a divine spark. And that ultimately the question is more important than the answer.

CHAPTER FOUR

The Holy Grail

We come now to the quest of our third hero, Parsifal, and to a creative artist, Richard Wagner, of whom we know much more than we know of the elusive Homer and the reclusive Virgil. In fact, for the last twelve years of Wagner's life, we know what he was doing and thinking almost from minute to minute (we even know what he was dreaming from night to night), for all of this was recorded in the diaries of his second wife, Cosima, the daughter of Franz Liszt. And we should say from the start that not everything that we know about Wagner is edifying. He was a notoriously imperfect man. Perhaps that is why *Der Fliegende Holländer, Tannhäuser, Lohengrin, Tristan und Isolde, Die Meistersinger*, the four parts of *Der Ring des Nibelungen*, and the final *Parsifal* are all, in their several ways, quests – personal searches for integrity by a man who needed integrity more than most men.

With *Parsifal*, I'm straying from the usual path of these Robson lectures. I shall draw on some material that may be familiar, because I've probably spoken and written on Wagner more than on any other figure in the arts.[1] And I'm speaking on a subject not directly related to the field of Classics. More than that, I'm not at all sure that Professor Robson would have approved of my introducing Wagner into this series. I remember that, as was the prevailing case at the time, he rather strongly disapproved of that sometime Wagnerite (and sometime classicist), Friedrich Nietzsche. But it was expected of me that one of the Robson lectures concern itself with opera, and perhaps with Wagnerian opera, however much music drama might differ in mode from hexameter epic. And because the two genres cannot, as George Steiner puts it, 'be heard in the same performative register,'[2] I shall have to consider, possibly to the discomfiture of both classicists and Wagnerians, the similarities in dissimilar modes. Perhaps the only real continuity will be provided, once again, by my personal responses to the three artists – for I have been deeply affected by each of them.

In *Parsifal* Wagner looked within himself and, out of the dark and light he found there, wrote one last opera to forfend the evil and heal the hurt he saw within, to reconcile and to integrate. More than the *Odyssey* and the *Aeneid*, *Parsifal* is about what is irrational, fearful, destructive, and wonderful in the human psyche, what potential there can be activated, what wound there must be closed. Wagner's opera is a long process of draining away the evil and bringing together the good. And its central symbol, the symbol of healing and integration, is the Holy Grail, the most famous object in all the literature of heroic questing.

Questing is in part questioning, and the pivotal moment in the long Parsifal tradition is the asking of the question. In the *Perceval* of Chrétien de Troyes, where the hero is schooled in chivalric service to others, the question he must ask is 'Whom does the Grail serve?' In the *Parzifal* of Wolfram von Eschenbach, where the hero finds himself related to virtually all the important characters he meets, the question is 'Uncle, what is it that causes your pain?' In Wagner, who attached less importance to the question but, placing it at the beginning not at the end of the quest, brought the old sources together in new and insightful ways, the hero asks, rather surprisingly, 'Who is the Grail?' I'll begin by asking, 'What is the Grail?' The four questions are related.

I'll have to go into Wagner's sources more than I did with Virgil (and more than was possible with Homer), and I should admit at this point that I'm hardly an authority on the extraordinarily complex tradition of the Grail legends. I've read Jessie Weston and Roger Loomis, but most of those who will read this book will know Malory's *Morte d'Arthur* and Tennyson's *Idylls of the King* better than I. In any case, we must begin by looking back several centuries before Tennyson, even a century or more before Malory, to a time when the Grail had no Arthurian and indeed no Christian significances.

What is the Grail? The word may have originally designated not, as we might expect, a cup but, as Western etymology might indicate, a dish or even, according to Hebrew, Arabic, and Persian etymologies, a stone. In early Celtic traditions it seems to have been a cauldron, and then again a cornucopia. Cultures from Spain to India have claimed as their own the sacred object we read of in the Grail sources, and there has been an astonishing amount of theorizing about that object's nature, shape, and origin.[3]

The best agreement we can come to about the Grail is to say that it was a very precious and possibly prehistoric life-giving object that – in Chrétien and Wolfram, who give us our oldest surviving versions of the legend – is kept in a virtually inaccessible castle by the wounded king of a wasted land. It awaits the arrival of an innocent youth who will, after an initial failure to grasp its meaning, return to ask the question that will heal the king and restore his kingdom. Meanwhile, it produces food and drink mysteriously for those who preserve it, and the mere sight of it is sufficient to keep even the oldest votary alive for seven days.

Though we no longer accept Jessie Weston's argument that this marvellous talisman was originally the object of veneration in a Near Eastern pre-Christian fertility ritual, there is little question among scholars that the Grail in the romances has antecedents that are older than, and sometimes even opposed to, Christianity. But by at least the twelfth century, and very likely earlier, the Grail was Christianized. In Chrétien's twelfth-century French romance *Perceval* or *Le Conte du Graal*, the Grail is a dish-shaped vessel of pure gold, streaming with light, bedecked with jewels, carried in procession and used to convey the eucharistic Host to its oldest attendant. It is in Chrétien that we first read of the innocent young Perceval who sees the shining Grail in its mysterious castle. Perceval has been reared by his mother in the Forest Desolate in Wales, kept far from human contact so as to prevent his becoming a knight like his two elder brothers, who have fallen in battle. Perceval's father has died of grief at the loss of those two sons. And his mother dies, too, after the sheltered Perceval sees five knights riding through the forest, takes them for God and his angels, and leaves home to learn chivalry at the court of King Arthur.

Perceval's story, intertwined in the sources with the story of the more worldly Gawain, has often been taken allegorically as a series of initiatory stages in the path towards knowing and loving God. Chrétien's young knight, gradually progressing to an understanding of what the Grail might mean, has a pronounced mystical bent, as is clear when he loses himself in contemplation of three drops of blood from a wounded goose streaming on white snow; they remind him of his spiritual love for the beautiful maiden Blanchefleur. (Chrétien is as important a figure in the development of the medieval code of courtly love as he is in the tradition of the Holy Grail.)

But Chrétien died leaving his *Perceval* unfinished. His hero gets no further in his quest than an encounter in a forest, on Good Friday, with a wise old hermit who is his maternal uncle. So the source most important for Wagner's opera, clearly based on Chrétien but completing his story, is the early-thirteenth-century Middle High German epic *Parzifal* by Wolfram von Eschenbach, the Bavarian minstrel whom the young Wagner put on the stage, as a baritone, in his opera *Tannhäuser*. Wagner was less than patient with Wolfram's epic because it traces no meaning in the events it narrates.[4] But there is no question that it is a true classic of the Middle Ages – a lively, lusty, wonderful thing, in rhymed couplets that fill sixteen books. And the Grail, when Wolfram's Parzifal first glimpses it in its elusive castle, is something rather different from what it was in Chrétien, and more mysterious still. Though it is carried before young Parzifal as part of a splendid ceremonial feast, the youth seems hardly to see it, or the author to know precisely what it is. Wolfram calls it the *Wunsch* (perhaps, 'the perfection') of Paradise, in both root and branches. That makes it sound like Virgil's Golden Bough, but later, in the exact centre of Wolfram's poem, when Parzifal meets the wise old hermit on Good Friday, that maternal uncle describes the Grail as a stone: it is called Lapsit Exillis, which is to say, perhaps, 'precious stone' (*lapis exilis*) or 'stone fallen from heaven' (*lapis* or *lapsit ex caelis*). It has oracular powers: around its edges magic writing comes and goes. (I've often thought that Stanley Kubrick and Arthur C. Clarke must have derived from Wolfram's stone that great stone slab that, in their film *2001: A Space Odyssey*, appears on earth or in space whenever the human race is ready for its next evolutionary step.)

Whatever it may be, Wolfram's stone, like Chrétien's dish, has been Christianized. Every Good Friday, the hermit tells Parzifal, a dove descends from heaven to place the eucharistic Host upon it.

Then there is a third source that extends the Christian dimensions of the myth still further – the thirteenth-century poem *Joseph d' Arimathie* by the pious Burgundian knight Robert de Boron.[5] Here the Grail becomes, and stays forever after, a cup. Joseph of Arimathea was the disciple in the four gospels who asked Pontius Pilate for the dead body of Jesus, took it down from the cross, and buried it in the tomb he had made for himself. In Robert's poem, Joseph of Arimathea has become a Roman decurion; he has preserved the cup Jesus used at the Last Supper and caught in it the blood that streamed from Jesus' side when it was pierced on the cross. The famous abbey at Glastonbury developed this identification into one of the perennial Grail legends. Though the English Channel seems hardly to exist in the Grail stories, where questing knights ride easily overland from Brittany to Britain,[6] the Glastonbury legend told how Joseph of Arimathea brought the cup by ship across the channel to Glastonbury Tor, to the lake island of Avalon that would later be associated with King Arthur, and buried it there – whence a miraculous stream of blood issued from the ground, while Joseph's staff, planted in the earth, became a thorn tree that, like Virgil's Golden Bough in mid-winter, blossomed every Christmas.

Some years ago I visited Glastonbury ('Jerusalem in England's green and pleasant land'), not by ship or chariot of fire but by ordinary Britrail. I saw the spot still called Chalice Well or Blood Spring. I knelt in the ruined abbey at the site of the tombs of Arthur and Guinevere, and plucked a spray from the thorn tree grafted from Joseph of Arimathea's staff. That spray stayed fresh in my room at London House all the time I wrote my book on Virgil's *Aeneid*. (It was, among talismans, the closest I ever came to the Golden Bough.) But I did not see Joseph's cup at Glastonbury, or in Wales, or anywhere else I quested for it. What was true in the Middle Ages is still true today: we must all find the Grail for ourselves, and not everyone is destined to find it.

For centuries across Europe tales were told about the cup being sighted now here, now there.[7] It was a time when faith was as much a matter of images and symbols as it was of dogma, when everything in life was seen as analogous to a spiritual reality, when travelling on pilgrimages and venerating sacred objects, especially relics of the Passion of Christ, were common practice for both king and subject. In the treasuries of European churches today we can still see relics by the hundreds of the Passion of Christ, authenticated only by the veneration of centuries but preserved in such beautiful shrines as La Sainte-Chapelle in Paris, which Saint Louis built, when he was king of France, to house the crown of thorns. The Grail stories grew out of the same age that saw the construction of the great Gothic cathedrals, out of the same astonishing faith and the same mythic impulse.[8]

What the Grail stories offered was a heterodox alternative to the sacramental liturgy of the medieval Church. In the ages of faith, any believer could, if he fasted and did penance, receive the Body and Blood of Christ under the simple forms of bread and, in some eras, wine – the forms that Jesus had used at the Last Supper. But medieval Christians, with their love of relics and their lively imaginations, responded powerfully to the ideal, expressed not by their priests but by their poets, of finding the very cup Jesus had used at that Supper, the very cup that had caught his precious blood as he hung upon the cross. Surely that cup was preserved somewhere, in some incredibly beautiful chapel inaccessible to ordinary men. Surely only the most perfect knights and heroes could ever find it.

As the tradition grew, neither fully accepted nor rejected by ecclesiastical authority, mythic ideas came to cluster around it: the Grail itself calls those who will serve it; it reveals itself when least expected, and only to those it chooses; the man who is strengthened by the sight of it, and partakes of the nourishment it provides, is invincible in battle, and he battles only for good; the man who is called by the Grail has to remain chaste while he serves it, and so long as he is chaste a Grail knight can work miracles. These aspects of the Grail owe something to the writings of Saint Bernard of Clairvaux, who traced the various stages a mystic passes through in the quest for perfection. They may also owe something, as can be intimated from our previous considerations, to Virgil, whose Golden Bough reveals itself only to, and can be plucked only by, the man called by Fate to find it.

Though Perceval is the earliest quester for the Grail in the sources, stories came to be told of others – Lancelot and Galahad and Gawain and Borhert. A thirteenth-century *Queste del Saint Graal*, the main source for Malory, tells how Sir Gawain fails on the quest because he does not seek the help of divine grace, while the devout Perceval and Bohert, when they find the Grail, are given special revelations. In the *Queste*, and thereafter, the most privileged knight of all is the pure young Sir Galahad, who can look directly into the Grail and perceive, if not the sight of God himself, mysteries no tongue can tell. As for his father, Sir Lancelot, perhaps the most memorable account of his failure was written in our century, in T.H. White's Camelot book *The Once and Future King*: Lancelot, who has sinned with Guinevere, tells her and Arthur, when they are all grown older, how he was unable even to see the Grail, when at last his expedition found it; bravest and strongest he still was, but he was no longer chaste, and he could work no more miracles, and when he found the holiest of sights, he could not see it.

Inevitably, in a fourteenth-century Europe that lost its ideals, the story was told that, because knights-errant were no longer worthy, the Grail cup vanished, leaving the world to wither and waste, awaiting its end. This became a symbol for our materialistic age in this century's most famous English poem, *The Waste Land* of T.S. Eliot. And that brings us to the wounded Grail king, and the spear.

Wagnerians will by now have wondered that, in all of this talk of a dish or a stone that became a cup, I've said nothing of a spear. For in Wagner the Grail may be said to be both a cup and a spear: the two objects have been brought together by angels to the first Grail king, Titurel, and they keep their mystic power of life and healing only when they are venerated together. The two objects may well have been symbolically related in pre-Christian traditions long before the medieval Grail legends,[9] but there is nothing in Wagner's sources or in Christian iconography to indicate that the Holy Grail was both cup and spear. There is of course the spear that pierced Jesus' side as he hung on the cross; fragmentary relics of that spear have been venerated across Europe for centuries. But that spear was never thought, through all the ages when the Grail legend was developing, to be part of the Grail.

And there is another spear in the tradition, as early as Chrétien and Wolfram: the castle where their naive youth first sees the Grail is the castle of a king who has been wounded by a heathen's spear. The king has pursued a love not allowed him by the writing on the Grail, and the wound, in his reproductive organs,[10] will not heal. And as the kingdom of the unfertile king withers around him to a waste land, he fishes daily in a lake beside his castle. (This might be thought to signify his patient searching of the waters of his unconscious for the sign that will restore fertility to himself and his land, but neither Chrétien nor Wolfram is the sort to venture such interpretations.) Wolfram gives this Fisher King a name: Anfortas (perhaps, 'infirm'). Wagner will use the alternate Amfortas (perhaps, 'brave love'), for the word *amor* was enscribed on the kings's shield when he first went bravely into battle.

Now we must add some details to our central Grail story. In Chrétien (and, with variations, in Wolfram), when our innocent youth sees the procession in the castle of the Fisher King, a beautiful boy carries the spear that has wounded the king, and a beautiful girl carries the 'Wunsch' or stone or sacred object that no longer has the power to heal him. The wondering Perceval/Parzifal has been told by Gurnemanz, a nobleman who trained him in chivalry, not to ask questions, so he never inquires what the strange procession might mean. Then, when he awakes the next morning to find the castle deserted, a weeping maiden tells him that, had he asked the right question, the Fisher King would have been healed.

Wolfram then carries the story to its conclusion: a hideous woman named Cundrie, once malevolent but now turned helpful, announces that the letters that appear mysteriously on the sacred object have proclaimed Parzifal its new king. So it is that, accompanied by a shadow-figure (his suddenly introduced half-black half-brother Feirefiz) and by an anima-figure (the ambivalent Cundrie), Parzifal finds the castle again, asks the question ('Uncle, what is it that causes you pain?'), and thereby heals the pierced Fisher King, who, like the hermit, has turned out to be a maternal uncle. Parzifal then becomes king himself.

Jungians who trace archetypal patterns in mythic stories have a mother-lode to mine in Wolfram. In addition to the pattern we have found in our other quests, Wolfram, influenced perhaps by the medieval iconography of the pierced heart, has a name for his hero's mother – Herzeloyde (heart's sorrow) – and he derives his hero's name, not entirely convincingly, from Old French *perce à val*, 'pierced down through the middle.'[11] In his *Parzifal* the 'pierced' hero finds the talismanic object that *one* of his maternal uncles has explained for him, and heals, by asking the question, the *other* maternal uncle, pierced by a spear.

It is time at last to turn to Wagner, for it is with the spear that Wagner made his most remarkable change in the legendary materials. He made the two spears in the legends one: his King Amfortas is wounded in the side by the very spear that had pierced the side of Jesus on the cross. And Wagner added that spear to the cup as part of the Grail. In Wagner the Holy Grail has begun to lose its power to strengthen and heal because the spear has been separated from the cup, stolen away by the forces of evil. And instead of writing on a stone, which Wolfram would have provided, Wagner has the voice of Jesus cry to Parsifal from the cup for the restoration of the spear.

This was a bold addition to the legend, and Wagner thought long and hard before he made it.[12] It is clearly intended to be significant, for it is presented to us in musical terms in the first page of the score. *Parsifal* opens with a hushed, long-spanned, chant-like melody shaped by the words of Jesus at the Last Supper ('Take this my body, take this my blood'). It is played first by the string section in solemn unison, and then intoned by a radiant solo trumpet supported by three luminous woodwinds. (Claude Debussy, who had no patience with the suffering characters in Wagner's text, was nonetheless astonished by what he heard synaesthetically in the music as stained-glass-window effects. For me, that trumpet sound is not stained glass but silver, and I've always thought it the most beautiful instrumental touch in all of Wagner's work, a moment when anyone searching for the Grail might catch a glimpse of it.)

But soon Wagner breaks his long Grail melody into three separate musical motifs. The first, curving section indicates the cup, and the last, thrusting fragment is associated with the spear, while the sorrowing mid-section becomes the theme of suffering – the suffering that comes on all of the characters in the drama because the spear has been separated from the cup. So at the start of his opera Wagner states, in a musical theme shaped by the words of Jesus, what his revision of the old legends might mean: there is suffering in the world because of the separation of the cup and the spear, because of the severing of what they represent.

Some contemporary medievalists object that Wagner wilfully spoiled Chrétien and Wolfram when he adapted them. But two intuitive Virgilians, W.F. Jackson Knight and Robert Cruttwell,[13] have felt that Wagner, in *Parsifal* as earlier in *Tristan*, thought his way past his Christian sources to the original meaning of the myths. Certainly, in his conflation of so many elements in the sources, he recaptured much of their mythic feeling. Roger Loomis says that an initiate of the old Celtic mysteries, if transported suddenly to New York, 'might witness a performance of Wagner's *Parsifal* and feel that among the appalling riddles of modern life here was at last something that in part he could comprehend.'[14] Lucy Beckett, author of a fine analysis of Wagner's opera, says that 'there is not a single Grail text discussed in [Loomis's] *Arthurian Literature in the Middle Ages* ... that does not somewhere strengthen or support the edifice Wagner constructed from Wolfram [and] Chrétien.'[15]

Wagner, who always wrote his own texts, shaped his mass of mythic material into an immense three-act symmetrical pattern, so that the incidents of Act III recapitulate those of Act I, with the discord resolved, as in a sonata form, after the conflict and illumination of Act II. In the course of this, he vastly simplified the cast of characters. His young hero rightly says, 'I had many names, but now I have forgotten them all,' for Wagner's Parsifal is the pure knight called, in various sources, Perceval, Parzifal, Peredur, Gawan, Galahad, Borhert, and other names as well. Wagner's kindly old Gurnemanz is a combination of two patriarchal characters in the tradition – the noble mentor who introduces the hero to chivalry and the nameless hermit who is his maternal uncle. And Wagner's Kundry is a remarkable amalgamation of at least four women from within the tradition and of several from beyond it. She is the beautiful Condwiramours (*conduire amour*) who first introduces young Parzifal to sexual experience; Sigune, his cousin, who explains his name to him and reproaches him for not asking the question; Cunnaware, the sorrowing maiden who never laughed till she met him; and of course the Grail messenger Cundrie, a Loathly Damsel on a mule when she appears malevolently, benevolent when she comes on horseback. Wagner's composite Kundry thus becomes an ambivalent anima-figure who has the power to destroy the knightly hero but who, once her evil power is defeated, can aid him on his quest.[16]

Wagner's Amfortas, unlike the wounded king in the sources, does not fish in the Grail castle's lake. He washes his wound in it. Wagner suspected that Chrétien had misunderstood fisher (*pêcheur*) for sinner (*pécheur*). Wagner also, for obvious reasons, transferred the wound of Amfortas to his side. Finally, for the wounding of his Sinner King, an incident largely undeveloped in the sources, Wagner wanted an evil figure. He borrowed for this purpose a personage from the Grail legends of Gawan – the eunuch magician Klingsor. In the sources, Gawan attacks Klingsor's castle, breaks its evil spell, and releases its captive women, among them yet another Kundry figure, the temptress Orgeluse.

If all of this has been confusing – and I don't doubt that it has – we can simplify it now by running through the story as Wagner tells it.

When the curtains part on Act I of *Parsifal*, we are high in the mountains of medieval Spain, the boundary between Christian and Moor, and a convenient setting for depicting legends that developed in both East and West. It is dawn in a forest clearing near Monsalvat, the castle in which the Grail cup is kept. The old knight Gurnemanz kneels in morning prayer with four young charges he is training in chivalry. They await the arrival of their king, Amfortas, who has been dealt an incurable wound and will come soon to assuage his pain in the lake that lies in view. But first they hear the approaching hoofbeats of the steed that carries the Wild Rider – a sinister figure who hurtles into the clearing and falls to the ground. The rider is the woman Kundry, come with balsam from Arab lands to alleviate the suffering of Amfortas. The king, borne in on his litter, bends in pain to thank her, and is carried away. She laughs in despair.

The young squires have seen Kundry before, and feared her and her terrible laugh, and now they clamour that *she* is the cause of all the sorrows that have come upon the castle. But wise old Gurnemanz rebukes them. Kundry's unexpected appearances, he says, always bring good. In a long narration, he tells how Kundry first appeared years before when they were bulding the castle to preserve two sacred objects once brought to King Titurel – the cup from which Jesus drank at the Last Supper and the spear that pierced his side when he hung on the cross. They have summoned knights from far and near to preserve them, and to do good deeds through their mystic power.

Among those who came to serve, Gurnemanz tells us, was Klingsor. He was turned away, for he was unable to remain chaste, even when, in desperation, he castrated himself. Unable to serve the Grail, Klingsor resolved to destroy it. He built his own castle in Arab lands across the mountains, mastered evil arts, and created a garden of flowering women to lure the knights away from the service of the Grail. One by one, the knights began to desert. Titurel grew old and sad, and retired to his mausoleum to live out his last days in solitude as the Grail's oldest votary, kept alive by the sight of it. The rule of the castle he left to his son Amfortas.

So young Amfortas, brave in his love, sallied forth with the Grail spear as his weapon to defeat Klingsor. But in Klingsor's magic garden he was met by, and bewitched by, a woman of incredible beauty. As he lay in her arms, he suddenly felt a stab of pain in his side. Klingsor had grasped the Grail spear, wounded Amfortas with it, and vanished. Amfortas returned to his castle, suffering from a wound that would not heal, and the Grail cup, without its spear, began to lose its power.

But, Gurnemanz tells the squires as they listen in wonder, there is some hope for the knights. One time when Amfortas was kneeling alone before the cup, praying for forgiveness, the sacred object began to glow, and a voice from within it spoke the words the knights have remembered ever since:

Durch Mitleid wissend, der Reine Tor,
Harre sein' den ich erkor.

Through compassion made wise, the pure fool,
Wait for him. I have chosen him.

Gurnemanz's long story is suddenly interrupted. Someone has shot a swan circling over the lake. All life is sacred at Monsalvat. No one can imagine who has dared kill the swan. Amfortas himself had sighted it while washing in the lake, and had taken heart, thinking it a good omen. The knights soon find the offender – not much more than a boy, all but speechless and completely unconscious of having done anything wrong. But when he sees the white swan pierced by his arrow, its snowy plumage spotted with blood, his eyes fill with tears. He breaks his bow and throws it away. They question him. He doesn't know his father's name. He himself has been called many names, but he has now forgotten them all. He only remembers his mother's name – Herzeleide (heart's sorrow). Kundry breaks a long silence and cries out with the knowledge she seems intuitively to possess: Herzeleide has died of grief that her son has left her. The youth's reaction to this is uncommonly violent: he attacks Kundry, then falls into a faint from which she revives him.

Wagner's orchestra often tells us, in recurrent themes, what the characters on stage do not tell, or sometimes do not know. As Kundry wanders off into the forest, the orchestra plays the chromatic theme already associated with Klingsor, and we realize, if we hadn't suspected before, that she is the very woman Klingsor had used to lure Amfortas to his destruction. Yet her instinct to do good seems as strong as the force that uses her for harm.

The castle bells announce that it is noon. Old Gurnemanz has begun to hope that the primitive, nameless youth may be the *reine Tor*, the pure fool that the Grail cup promised would some-day come *durch Mitleid wissend*, made wise through compassion, to find the spear and restore to the Grail its power to heal. The old man puts his arm around the youth and leads him towards the castle of the Grail. The youth, beginning his quest, asks the question: 'Who is the Grail?'

Gurnemanz only says, 'If you are called, the knowledge will not be lost to you.'

Then, in one of Wagner's great moments, the music moves wondrously forward in step with the distant tolling bells, and the tall forest trees around the two figures change almost imperceptibly into the soaring vertical lines of a castle shaped like a Gothic cathedral. The youth exclaims that, though everything is changing around him, he himself hardly seems to be moving. Gurnemanz explains, with the words many of us like to apply to Wagner's immense suspended musical structures, 'Du siehst, mein Sohn – You see, my son, here time becomes space.'

But as the knights file in to stand at a round table, the youth does not understand what he sees – the stricken Amfortas unveiling the Grail cup at the command of his father Titurel, who is kept alive only by the sight of it; the castle growing dark till the only light comes from the cup that, like the stone in the sources, mysteriously produces bread and wine for the ceremony; the knights singing 'Take this my body, take this my blood,' their chant repeated by the silvery trumpet we heard in the prelude. At first, Amfortas is strengthened like the others: his face shines like a saint's as he elevates the cup and traces with it a cross in the air. Then, as the other knights partake of the bread and wine, Amfortas's wound breaks open, and the youth seems suddenly to feel the pain of that wound in his own side.

When the ceremony is over, and all have left, Gurnemanz asks the youth, 'Do you know what you saw?' The youth says nothing, and Gurnemanz, bitterly disappointed, sends him unceremoniously away. No one is there to hear a voice that, echoing through the room, quietly declares that the youth *is* the long-awaited *reine Tor*.

That first act is, in some conductors's hands, the longest act in the whole of operatic literature, and I've given something more than a précis of it. The second and third acts we can summarize more quickly.

In Act II Wagner presents us with a castle, a wounded king, and a landscape to oppose the castle, king, and landscape of the Grail's realm. We are in Klingsor's realm, across the mountains of Spain, in Arab lands. The eunuch Klingsor can see, in a great mirror, that he has by his magic drawn the youth of the first act into his flowery domain. He can see the Grail knights he has lured away rise up to defend him. He can see the youth valiantly slaying them. He calls up the Wild Rider of the first act – Kundry, whom he has used to lure the knights away. She tries to resist, as she always has before. We hear now that she has had many names and lived through several incarnations.

Under Klingsor's power, with a terrible laugh that turns to a wail of despair, Kundry attempts the youth's seduction. As she appears to him, mysteriously beautiful, she tells him his name – Parsifal – inverting the Persian *fal parsi* ('pure fool').[17] The magically animate flowers in Klingsor's garden become young girls who sing a kind of cradle song, and the youth remembers, 'Parsifal – once my mother called me that in a dream!' Kundry tells him how she saw him when he was a child at his mother's breast. And when he is filled with mother-longings, she gives him his first kiss.

Suddenly, with the dawning of sexual awareness within him, the youth, become a man, is fully conscious of the human condition, of its potential for goodness and evil, of the profound flaw and hurt in it. He thinks back to what he did not understand in that castle in the forest – the voice crying from the cup for the restoration of the spear, his own feeling that the pain of the wounded Amfortas was somehow in his own soul. And now that he has himself experienced the pain of Amfortas, he feels that he can heal him if he can find and restore the spear. As Kundry vac-

illates between her two natures – destructive and creative –
Klingsor rises in the background, poised to wound Parsifal with
the spear that had wounded Amfortas. But because he is pure the
youth can work miracles: he grasps the spear in its flight and
with it traces a cross in the air. Klingsor's castle disintegrates.

Then, in Act III, Wagner, in one of his massive recapitula-
tions, takes us back again to the castle of the Grail. Many years
have passed. The cup has all but lost its power, and old Titurel
has died. Parsifal has wandered through a waste land, carrying
the spear back to the cup. Now, on Good Friday, in a green valley, he and the reawakened Kundry meet amid flowers once more
– but these flowers seem to smile with the tears of redeemed
nature. Wise old Gurnemanz, now living the life of a hermit,
explains to the maturing hero and the ambivalent woman that,
on this day, when God forgave the world, repentant human tears
make the waste land blossom. Kundry, who in a previous life had
laughed at Christ carrying his cross, and whose terrible laughter
has always kept her from tears, now weeps like any human
being. She bathes Parsifal's feet and, as the Magdalen had done to
the feet of Jesus, dries them with her hair. As the orchestra
intones the incredibly lovely 'Good Friday Spell,' we get a sacramental moment to balance the ceremonial baptism of Walther's
song in *Die Meistersinger*. (The lyrical climax of both works
comes just before the scene change in Act III). Parsifal accepts
from Gurnemanz the baptism of water and the anointing of oil
that will make him a Christian and the Grail's new king.

The scene changes one last time. As in Act I, Parsifal hardly
seems to move at all as he passes through a landscape where time
becomes space. This time, however, he approaches the castle not
through a dark forest but through a radiant meadow. This time
Kundry accompanies him, for he has turned the evil potential in
her to good. This time the wise old Gurnemanz does not lead but
follows, for now Parsifal has come not as a youth who unthink-
ingly killed a swan but as a man who has come to know the flaw,
the hurt, in the world. This time the wounded Amfortas will be
healed, for Parsifal carries aloft the long-lost spear with which
he will make the Holy Grail, once more, complete and whole.
(I have often thought that the two contrasting journeys through

changing time and space, with Gurnemanz leading the way in Act I and with Parsifal leading in Act III, prompted Marcel Proust, on his quest for lost time, to name his two symbolic paths through memory the 'côté de Guermantes' and the 'côté de chez Swann.' Perhaps that is why, between those third and first volumes of his questing novel, Proust places the 'jeune filles en fleurs,' the flower maidens of Wagner's Act II.)

Parsifal enters the castle at the terrible moment when Amfortas exposes his bleeding wound and orders his knights to draw their swords and end his suffering. 'Only one weapon can heal the hurt,' Parsifal sings. He touches the spear-point to Amfortas's bleeding wound. 'Be purified,' he proclaims, 'whole and absolved. And blest be all your suffering, for it has made me wise. It has taught me compassion.' The words for compassion and wisdom are, of course, *Mitleid* and *Wissen*.

The bleeding stops. The whole enclosed space grows dark. Parsifal places the spear on the Grail stone, with the cup. The spear-point begins to glow, just as the cup always has at moments of unveiling. For a few moments, the only illumination is the light from the cup and the spear. The incredibly beautiful music that began the opera returns, more awe-inspiring even than before because the themes of the cup and the spear are no longer separated by the theme of suffering.

Then a ray of white light breaks from the dome, and the dove that, in the old legends, renewed the Grail's power every Good Friday appears, descends, and hovers over Parsifal's head. As Parsifal raises the cup and traces a cross in the air, the knights all kneel and open their arms upward to the light. Kundry sinks slowly to the ground – now, after all the centuries, released from her cycle of reincarnations. And innocent boys' voices, from the dome we cannot see, sing 'This is the greatest miracle of all. Redemption has come to the Redeemer.'

And as the last transcendent chord fades away every listener wonders, like an initiate at the mysteries, 'What does it all mean?'

I'm not sure that anyone has ever answered that question. Certainly the answers we have are widely divergent. Often the same person has changed his mind several times on the matter. The most famous of these is that young neo-pagan professor of Classics who spent his early years under the spell of Wagner, Friedrich Nietzsche. In 1877 he wrote to Wagner's wife Cosima, 'The glories *Parsifal* promises us can comfort us in all the matters where we need comfort.'[18] But after Wagner's death in 1883, Nietzsche said, without having heard any of the music, that he took it as a personal insult that the man he thought Aeschylus *redivivus* had written an opera replete with Christian sacramental symbols. In 1886, in a new preface to *Human, All Too Human*, he lamented that in *Parsifal* Wagner had forsaken his classic Greek ideals and – 'apparently most triumphant, but in truth a decaying, despairing decadent' – had sunk at the foot of the cross in an attempt to ingratiate himself with Europe's wealthy Christian rulers and bourgeoisie.

But the next year, when Nietzsche first heard the *Parsifal* prelude with its shining trumpet, he found to his amazement 'a sublime and extraordinary feeling ... an event of the soul ... an awful severity of judgement "from on high" which issues from an intimate understanding of the soul and sees through the soul, piercing it as with knives. And hand in hand with this goes a compassion for what has been perceived.' In effect Nietzsche was admitting, albeit in a private letter, that he had found in Wagner's work the motives of vision, wounding, and healing that were part of the Grail myths from the beginning. 'Only Dante is comparable,' he said, 'nobody else.'

Then that same year Nietzsche changed his mind again (or chose to express himself differently in a public pronouncement) when, in *The Genealogy of Morals*, he proclaimed *Parsifal* 'a work of perfidy ... a secret attempt to poison the suppositions of life ... a bad work ... an incitement to anti-nature ... an attempted assassination of basic ethics.'[19]

Opinions have varied ever since. Is Wagner's opera sacred or profane, moral or immoral, religious or anti-religious? Wagner himself called it a *Bühnenweihfestspiel*, a 'stage-consecrating festival play. Wagner's festival at Bayreuth was the stage it would consecrate, and it would be performed only there, in a proper atmosphere of reverence, by those who could properly perform it and for those who could properly understand it. But after a century of proper performances, at Bayreuth and elsewhere, is there anyone who really understands the last work of the master?

About the only certainty is that one cannot talk about *Parsifal* for any length of time without involving oneself in a tangle – a jungle – of contradictions. Deadly controversies luxuriate around Wagner's final statement like the animate flowers in Klingsor's magic garden. When I first read Homer, as a student at St Michael's College in the University of Toronto, Jacques Maritain said of Wagner's operas that they dull and debauch the eye, the ear, and the spirit. And when I was writing on Virgil in London, I spoke with Colin Davis, then the musical director of the Royal Opera, Covent Garden. Sir Colin was conducting *Tristan* and the *Ring* at that great house, and *Tannhäuser* at Bayreuth. He spoke warmly of his admiration for the radiant musical textures of *Lohengrin* and of his love for the genial humanity of *Meister-singer*. But, he told me, he was a deeply religious man, and he could not love, or admire, or even come to terms with *Parsifal*. Most of it he found questionable, and some of it positively repellent. We talked about it for some time. He listened carefully to what I had to say. But nothing I said could make any difference for him. *Parsifal* was, for both of those sensitive, high-minded, and intelligent men, simply beyond the pale.

But for many of us who have come to love it (and it took me some time to overcome my own misgivings[20]), *Parsifal* is not deadly but life-affirming. I can remember *Parsifal* performances where I watched, as usual, from an inexpensive seat in the upper reaches of the house, hovering there with the unearthly feeling, for long half-hours, of floating in an immense space, suffused with a sense of what Baudelaire felt when listening to Wagner – the sense of being suspended in an ecstasy compounded of joy and insight. I can remember, in Karlsruhe, in Bremen, in Rome, in New York, staggering out of the theatre after *Parsifal*, the music streaming through me, carried out of myself, seeing my experience – indeed, feeling that I was seeing all experience – at a higher level of awareness, unable to speak, put in touch with a power greater than myself. I became a kind of holy fool – like Mahler, who wrote, 'Emerging speechless from the Festspiel-haus, I realized that I had undergone the greatest and most soul-wrenching experience in my life, and that I would carry this experience with me for the rest of my days.' Like Hugo Wolf, who also stumbled out of the theatre, and sat by himself for hours with his face buried in his hands; who declared *Parsifal* 'by far the most beautiful and sublime work in the whole field of art,' and added, 'My whole being reels in the perfect world of this wonderful work, as if in some blissful ecstasy ... I could die even now.' Like Sibelius, who wrote, 'Nothing else in all the world had made so overwhelming an impression on me. All my innermost heartstrings throbbed.'[21]

There seems little question that Wagner in his final work has, as even Nietzsche came close to admitting, captured and conveyed something of the power and meaning the Grail legends once conveyed. And there *are* some approaches through his tangled forest to the Grail. One path for our day is, as I've indicated, via the archetypes of C.G. Jung and his disciples: the boy with the many names is the maturing male, the hero with a thousand faces passing from innocence to awareness, encountering his shadow (Amfortas in Act I), his anima (Kundry in Act II), and his Wise Old Man (Gurnemanz in Act III), and integrating all of these experiences in a mandala-symbol of the self (the Grail, restored to completeness in the final scene).[22]

Northrop Frye has observed that in the Grail myth psychic integration is achieved with the union of male and female principles, of the cup 'with female sexual affinities,' and the spear, 'its masculine counterpart.'[23] The emphasis on chastity, both in the sources and in Wagner's treatment of them,[24] is best understood not biologically but psychologically: the Grail knight vowing to keep chaste as he quests for the Grail is the myth's way of saying that a man in pursuit of the integration of his personality must not surrender to his inner femininity, his anima, one aspect of which is (as in Keats's 'La Belle Dame sans Merci') destructive. He must defeat this side of his inner feminine in order to release the anima's creative potential. Kept as an ideal, the feminine principle in a man is a source of strength; surrendered to, it can be psychologically destructive.

Wagner may well have anticipated these Jungian ideas. But in his own day he would likely have referred anyone looking for the meaning of his *Parsifal* to the writings of his contemporary Arthur Schopenhauer. For that pessimistic philosopher the essence of the world was a blind, irrational power (*Wille*, or will) that operates in brute nature in forces such as gravity, in animals as instinct, and in humans as endless, driving, insatiable longing. This longing, for Schopenhauer, is the source of all our pain. We can find no peace till we acknowledge it in our natures, deny it, and overcome it. All of this Wagner had already dramatized in the last act of *Tristan*. His Wotan had come to grips with it in the *Ring*. His Hans Sachs had seen deeply into it in *Die Meistersinger*. For each of these characters, the world, with all its beauty, was essentially flawed, full of longing and suffering and pain. And in *Parsifal* all the tormented characters cry out, far more than in the medieval sources, that they are suffering from endless longing. From this point of view, it is of *Wille*'s painful, insatiate longing that Parsifal first becomes aware when, at Kundry's kiss, he passes from youth to manhood.

But *Parsifal* takes us further than Wagner's earlier works, past Schopenhauer's metaphysics to his ethics, past *Wille* to *Mitleid* – another key term for the philosopher. *Mitleid* means 'empathy,' 'compassion,' 'suffering with.' Wagner's Grail knights have heard that healing will come to their suffering king with the advent of a pure fool 'made wise through *Mitleid*.' In Schopenhauer, the initial step towards overcoming *Wille*'s gravitational pull is a kind of selfless, spiritual purity. When a man is not driven by his own passion, he is able to feel the pain that others feel. He can even come to feel, through *Mitleid*, the sufferings of others in himself. That is how he finds himself.

Wagner's absorption in Schopenhauer (and Frye has suggested that, more than the Christian elements in the text, it was the Schopenhauer there that so infuriated Nietzsche[25]) eventually led him to Buddhism. Wagner was always interested in any doctrine of deliverance from suffering, and Buddhism is that doctrine *par excellence*. When in the midst of composing the *Ring* he first came under Schopenhauer's influence, he sketched a drama, *Die Sieger*, based on the Buddhist legend of Ananda, the themes of which (renunciation, reincarnation, and redemption) were eventually worked into *Parsifal*. Not incidentally, the first three truths of Buddhism – that all human existence is pain, that pain is caused by desire, and that the highest wisdom comes in renouncing that desire – virtually define the three acts of both *Parsifal* and the earlier *Tristan*.

There are any number of Buddhist elements in Wagner's last opera. Perhaps the best explanation of Wagner's Kundry lies not in any of the European sources, but in the story of the Indian woman Savitri in Wagner's sketch for *Die Sieger*: Savitri, like Kundry, experiences a series of reincarnations, but can never satisfy her longing until Buddha himself frees her from that longing. Buddha means 'the awakened,' and Buddhist illumination comes after an awakening from unconsciousness; so, in Wagner's first act, Parsifal and, in his last act, Kundry are each awakened to new illuminations after fainting into unconsciousness. But most of all it was the Buddhist teaching on compassion that Wagner was drawn to. He said near the end of his life that it was the need for compassion, feeling the sufferings of others in his unfeeling self, that compelled him to compose. His young Parsifal moves from compassion for the swan he has killed to compassion for the sufferings of Amfortas, of the Grail knights, of Kundry, and of the world itself. He feels their suffering within himself, and he heals their hurt.[26]

Arnold Toynbee has said that our century would be remembered not for the atom bomb but for the beginning of serious dialogue between Christianity and Buddhism. The theologian Hans Küng finds *Parsifal* a forward-looking work for that reason: 'Buddhist and Christian ways of thought converge in it ... Both Christianity and the Indian religion realize mankind's alienation, his decline, his need for redemption ... Both are troubled about the unspeakable suffering which results from man's own deeds and their consequences ... (and both) hope for a redemption which will bring enlightenment, knowledge, transformation, deliverance.'[27] Küng even speaks of Wagner as undertaking a historical experiment, a synthesis of Christian and Buddhist ways of thought, in his final work. Professor Emmet Robbins of the Classics department of this university once suggested to me that when, on Wagner's Good Friday, Kundry accepts baptism and so ends her cycle of suffering reincarnations, the implication is that Buddhism and Christianity have been reconciled.

As a classicist listening to *Parsifal*, I also remember the great moment in the parodos of Aeschylus's *Agamemnon*, when the chorus sings that *pathei mathos* ('man learns though suffering') is a law laid down by God. This is perhaps as close as Aeschylus comes to answering what Wagner thought was the *Parsifal* question: 'Why is there suffering in the world?' While he was writing *Parsifal* Wagner was reading not only Schopenhauer and Buddhist writings but Aeschylus as well, and he exclaimed in wonder over that great two-hundred-line chorus at the start of the *Agamemnon*, declaring it the finest thing he had ever read. *Pathei mathos* is an answer close to 'Durch Mitleid wissend.' We suffer so that we can learn and – Wagner adds – help others who are suffering.[28]

It must also be said that there are some less admirable ideas to be found beneath the philosophies of compassion and the beautiful musical surfaces of *Parsifal*. Wagner, a deeply flawed human being, never found in his life the peace, the resignation, the humanity he preached in his works. And it is all too easy to see the pamphleteering pronouncements he issued during the writing of *Parsifal* – pronouncements on race, religion, eugenics, socialism, and a score of other subects – mirrored in the opera's text. More than most composers, Wagner depended on ideas to power his creative energies, and this need grew stonger, and the ideas more dubious, as he aged.[29] Some of the ideas may have found expression in the music. Some of them, as is all too well known, contributed to the climate that produced Germany's Third Reich. That Wagner's legacy was misappropriated and misunderstood by the Nazis does not completely exonerate the composer. Ideas have consequences, and music, especially music as powerful as Wagner's, can lend persuasive support to them. But Wagner's ideas have also had a vast, century-long, positive influence (not as often acknowledged by his critics) on symbolist poets and impressionist painters, on our greatest composers, conductors, and stage designers, on our foremost novelists and dramatists. We have been slow to acknowledge his anticipation of some of the discoveries of this century's psychology. Wagner's is an influence far beyond that of any other artist of the past hundred years – an ambivalent legacy but a very important one.[30] If Wagner himself was sometimes a hateful man, deceitful, foolish, selfish, self-destructive and destructive,[31] it ought to be remembered that many of our greatest artists have been and are hateful and self-destructive. That is why they create. That is why their works are about healing. And that is why they can heal.

So, like the mysterious Grail itself, Wagner's final work is many things beneath its Christian surfaces. But I'd like finally to suggest, with some recent commentators, that *Parsifal* really is about what it seems to be about – Christianity.

Wagner's attitude towards Christianity was, for most of his life, hostile, and often aggressively hostile. (He was, for one thing, unsparing in his contempt for Catholic priests.) Christianity was the antithesis of all that he saw, through German Romantic eyes, as natural, pagan, classic, and Greek. He thought it particularly antagonistic to art, because it taught man to mistrust his body and his emotions, and to feel shame and guilt. He did admit that under a Christian ethic some arts had flourished, but only in isolation and not, as in classic Greek drama, in interdependence. Christianity, he said, had put art on the periphery, not at the centre, of life, and nowhere was this more true than with the theatre. In the theatre of Dionysus in classic Athens, the young Wagner rightly observed, a dramatic presentation was a religious event: on the feast of the god, in the presence of the god, an Athenian saw his own personal experience illuminated in his ancestral myths, and the god spoke to him through the masked actors in the theatre. But in nineteenth-century Europe, theatre was only a commercial entertainment for the well-to-do, utterly devoid of any religious significance. A German saw and heard nothing to nurture his spirit when, on any night that suited his convenience, he went to the theatre. 'We relegate the theatre,' Wagner said, 'to so low a place in public esteem that it becomes the business of the police to forbid it to touch on religious themes. And that tells us a good deal about both our religion and our art.'[32]

On the other hand, Wagner admired the founder of Christianity. He thought that in his early dramatic sketch *Jesus of Naza-*

reth he had discovered the real Jesus, a man of compassion. In his later years he found Christianity's symbols, especially its sacraments, resonant and beautiful, even if the Christian churches had, he said, buried Jesus's true message under a mass of irrelevant dogma. Wagner's role as reformer (the word that musicologists have inevitably used of him) was clear to him. First, in an age of materialism and commercialism, the theatre needed (in the word he himself inevitably used) redeeming. He brought a new kind of drama to his stage at Bayreuth, an art form in which – for the first time, he said, since classic Greece – all the arts interacted and profoundly significant myths were dramatized. Second, in an age Wagner thought devoid of spiritual values, Christ too needed redeeming. It is not for nothing that the last words of *Parsifal* are 'redemption to the Redeemer.' European Christianity had preserved the cup but, in Wagner's rearrangement of the sources, lost the spear – preserved the symbolism but lost the purpose –of its Founder. And when, from the cup, the voice of that Founder cries out to the pure young hero to rescue the lost spear, the implication is that Christianity, for all its legendary beauty, has been almost mortally wounded. All it has left are its symbols. Its enemies have largely triumphed.

But there is hope for it. From without. From a non-Christian who learns to see clearly into its symbols, who can grasp them, save them, restore them to potency. Wagner's Parsifal, we note with some surprise, is not a Christian at all. He accepts baptism only when, in the last act, he is ready to wield himself the symbols of Christianity in order to help others. He is, like all of Wagner's protagonists, a figure for Wagner himself at the time of writing.

Here is a revealing statement Wagner made during the writing of *Parsifal*: 'When religion becomes artificial, art has a duty to rescue it, by showing that the mythic symbols which religion would have us believe literally true are actually figurative. Art can idealize those symbols, and so reveal the profound truths they contain.'[33] *Parsifal* attempts to show the figurative truth in Christianity's symbols, and the healing power in them.

Wagner named the home he built at Bayreuth 'illusion's peace' (Wahnfried) – a strange name till one recalls that Hans Sachs in

Die Meistersinger sings how a true artist can use illusion (*Wahn*) constructively, in the interests of peace. Wagner may never have subscribed wholeheartely to the dogmas of Christianity, but at the end of his life he did come to see its insights as immensely valuable. Christianity became for him the most beautiful of myths – an illusion, perhaps, but a grand illusion with the power, in its symbols, to heal and inspire. He turned to it when he saw nineteenth-century society caught up in an advancing wave of materialism. Only two weeks before his death he wrote to his scholarly friend Heinrich von Stein, 'If we cannot save the world from its curse, we can at least present it with the possibility of saving itself, through symbols that will direct it to deep insight.'[34] In short, the Parsifal that appears in Wagner's last act is a projection of Wagner himself in his last years, as much as the Dutchman and Tannhäuser spoke for him in his early years, much as the other heroes are figures for himself at various stages in his life as he felt his way, failing in his life but succeeding in his art, towards awareness, fulfilment, and illusion's peace.

Many people who love *Parsifal* will say that that is not explanation enough. One of those would be Cambridge's Lucy Beckett, who ends her perceptive book on Wagner's opera with a strong claim for its being implicitly and explicitly Christian. She goes so far as to say that Wagner in *Parsifal* anticipated by almost a century the dynamic theology that we have today, when Christians, following Karl Barth, are less interested in a transcendent God and more open to a God immanent in the concerns, and especially in the sufferings, of others.[35]

Another who would tell me I do not see deeply and simply enough into *Parsifal* is Etienne Gilson, that historian of the Middle Ages who taught for many years at St Michael's College and co-founded the Institute of Mediaeval Studies there. A rigorous intellectual and a profoundly devout man, he nonetheless wept openly in the midst of a lecture at the thought of Wagner's medieval myth in music, and said that nothing in art meant more to him than Parsifal's purity, steadfastness, and sense of compassion for the sufferings of others. *Parsifal*, he once told me quietly, 'is the greatest of operas, highest in the heaven of heavens.' He did not think it unscholarly to ignore Nietzsche's – and Wagner's

– presumptions and listen to *Parsifal* as he saw it, as an incredibly beautiful realization in sound of one of Christendom's fairest legends.

If, then, the mazes of this discussion have only complicated Wagner's last opera for you, you have only to open the score to page one and read, or put side one on your turntable and listen, or sit in the darkened auditorium and wonder. That opening music still does, as Nietzsche said it did, cut through the soul like a knife. Whatever questionable ideas went into its making, the finished work of art has a life of its own and a truth of its own. As we read, hear, or watch one of mankind's profoundest myths unfold, the music cuts through the soul so much that, at the close, when the spear is restored to the cup, one feels – as in all of Wagner's endings, but most powerfully in this instance – that all this is really about oneself.

Perhaps then I can end with the simplest of explanations. Wagner's *Parsifal* is not just about the man who wrote it but about any of us who is human and flawed and suffering, about the need any of us has for inner reconciliation, integration, purpose, and peace. That is to say, it is truly in the tradition of the quest. The timeless, spaceless forest-castle we approach without even moving is our inner self. The sufferings of Amfortas and Kundry, the self-destructive hatred of Klingsor, the quiet wisdom of Gurnemanz, are part of any of us. Parsifal's call to a chaste – that is, selfless – compassion is our own vocation selflessly to heal ourselves. The integration, within the soul, of male and female principles symbolized by the spear and the cup is the miracle all of us are called to work within ourselves.

So Wagner, simplifying his French and German sources, has the innocent youth led through the forest of his unconscious to the castle deep within it but not really distinct from it – he has that potential knight at the start of his quest ask, not '*What* is the Grail?' but '*Who* is the Grail?' The Grail that calls out to be redeemed, rescued, restored to wholeness is, to answer Wolfram's question, 'what causes *your* pain.' To answer Chrétien's question, *you* are the one 'whom the Grail serves.'

Who is the Grail? You are the Grail.

CHAPTER FIVE

The Eternal Feminine

Invited by the Robson Classical Lecture committee to add a fourth, written, chapter to the three delivered orally on the quest in Homer, Virgil, and Wagner, I entertained various possibilities. Other quests in Greek and Latin literature – the mythic voyage of the Argonauts as told by Pindar and Apollonius of Rhodes, the philosophical quest for ideal justice culminating in the myth of Er in Plato's *Republic,* the comic questing of Aristophanes' heroes for peace during the Peloponnesian war – all of these lay somewhat beyond my area of expertise. I had taught them all, but not lived with them so much as with my three chosen works.

I cast my sight wider, and thought of those questing works I have known for many years and returned to many times – works as vast as *The Divine Comedy,* as insightful as *Don Quixote,* as picaresque as *Tom Jones,* as frightening as *Heart of Darkness,* as homely and wise as *Huckleberry Finn.* All of them are rooted in myth and, in their ways, are successors to the tradition begun by Homer. But after some reflection I told myself that there was little I could contribute to an appreciation of them beyond my personal responses. Mozart's mythic *The Magic Flute* was of course a possiblity for this opera-lover, but my views on that Enlightenment journey are available elsewhere.

Goethe, who wrote a sequel to *The Magic Flute* and may have found in it some of the fantastical feel that went into the second part of his *Faust,* was the man I have finally opted for. I have read *Faust* several times over the years. I have seen it (in an understandably condensed but nonetheless understandable version) in the Volkstheater in Vienna, and wondered about it often, even when reading Homer and Virgil or when listening to Wagner. I have some small acquaintance with the vast amount of scholarship written on it in English, and followed some of the leads therefrom into the vaster amounts of Goethian scholarship in German. I may have something to say about *Faust* that is new. But as Jacob Burckhardt once wrote to one of his students, 'What you are destined to discover in *Faust* you will have to discover intuitively. *Faust* is a genuine myth, i.e., a great primordial image, in which every man has to discover his own being and destiny in his own way.'[1] So what I say about Goethe's questing work will still be, largely, a personal response, the response of a man trained in the Classics.

A man trained in the Classics, with his imagination set free by *The Magic Flute* and *The Divine Comedy*, his inner anxieties quickened by Conrad, and his sense of fun enlivened by reading Cervantes, Fielding, and Mark Twain, will perhaps first think of *Faust*, not in terms of the early pages where a compact is made between an old philosopher and an enterprising devil, but in terms of those remarkable hundred pages in Part Two – the Classical Walpurgisnacht that spins out like a dream in the Vale of Tempe and in 'the rocky inlets of the Aegean Sea' (Act II), and the ensuing Helen episode that moves from 'the palace of Menelaus in Sparta' to a Gothic medieval castle watched over by a Greek Argonaut (Act III). Those 'classic' pages are meant to be a chimerically Romantic vision of classical Greece – hence the appearance of the sharp-eyed Greek sailor in a fairy-tale German castle and of an Arcadia the Goethian exuberance of which would have astonished Theocritus and perhaps embarrassed Virgil.

What a phantasmagorical trip it all is! I hope that I may be allowed to describe it as the restless dream I might have had on the night before my last examination in Honour Classics fifty years ago here at the University of Toronto. For in the days of Professor Robson, we who were enrolled in that most demanding of honour courses were expected to write a dozen final examinations in Greek and Latin at the end of each academic year, and I for one stayed sane by letting my imagination run riot occasionally.

In the dream, I'm an alchemical bit of artificial life enclosed in a glass bubble. (This is perhaps an unconscious presentiment of the examination on neo-Platonism I'm scheduled to write in the morning.) My name, Homunculus, is masculine, but I'm not really sure of my sex. I seem to have been born as pure intellect (which is pretty much what I feel I must become for the remainder of the examination period). I've been invented in a Gothic laboratory by a single-minded graduate student, Faust's laboratory assistant, Wagner. There is of course no connection between this lowly figure and the Bayreuth master of our previous chapter, who was only a boy at the time this part of Goethe's *Faust* was published. Wagner the composer of *Parsifal* was a quester, a bold explorer of subconscious realms. Wagner the unimaginative sorcerer's apprentice in *Faust* is everything Faust himself might have remained, musty with book dust, had he not gone on his questing adventures.

Hovering with that laboratory assistant over my test-tube birth is that most Gothic of devils, Mephistopheles. He is amazed as he sees the gleam inside my laboratory vial, and charmed to see my substance stirring into life. I wake and, precociously gifted with speech, accept Wagner as my father and Mephistopheles as my cousin.[2] My dream has become an *Alptraum*!

I wonder what I can do with my new life, and find to my amazement that my glass bubble can fly, which I proceed to make it do, hovering over Faust, who, like a true questing hero, is asleep with dreams of Leda and the swan – that is to say, with dreams of the begetting of the woman who has led him ever onwards, Helen of Troy.

Adept at the Classics, I can discern Faust's classicizing dreams, and this irks Mephistopheles, who only knows his German Gothickry. Presumptuously I order the devil to wrap the sleeping Faust in his academic cloak, and I light the way for the philosopher and his demonic companion out of the darkness of medieval Germany, south to the fields of Pharsalia. Wagner I leave peremptorily behind.

All is at peace in the field where Pompey once clashed with Julius Caesar. The moon floods the landscape with silver light. Faust awakes and asks for Helen. Mephisto takes leave of him to follow his own amorous interests in this landscape he has never known. I discover that I can reunite the two if need be by flashing my light: my lantern-like bubble rings like a bell when it lights up.

But who in the dream can tell Faust anything of Helen's whereabouts? Oedipus's Sphinx is there, and Odysseus's Sirens, but those potentially dangerous females do not easily reveal their secrets. It is finally Chiron the fatherly centaur who, at the river Peneus with its nymphs and swans, canters up, takes Faust on his back and, with tales of the adventures he has known, trots forth on the quest to find Helen. He tells Faust – and it is something he says the average Classics professor needs to be told too from time to time – that mythic figures never age, that Helen remains forever young. (Faust himself, since the initial transformation consequent on his pact with the devil, has remained vigorous and youthful – thirty, by common critical consent – and will stay at that age till his drama reaches its final act.)

Meanwhile, I seem to be tossing in my sleep: the god Seismos has caused the Vale of Tempe to quake, and (my Homer examination was last week) I witness before my very eyes Homer's famous simile of the cranes fleeing winter and the endless rains to do battle with the Pygmies. Then my dream, as dreams will, conflates the cranes of Homer with the cranes that avenged the death of the lyric poet Ibycus. (But then throughout this strange dream Goethe has concealed any number of learned allusions, and I remember, as I clutch my pillow, that Goethe's friend Schiller wrote a famous poem on the cranes of Ibycus.)

Mephistopheles has found the sacred oaks of Greece distinctly lacking in the tang of Harz mountain pitch – his 'favourite scent except for brimstone.' He has also proved to be something of a medieval prude, a devil disturbed by the innocent nakedness of Greece's nymphs. He much prefers the vulgarity of the rag-tag witches he conjured up in the other Walpurgisnacht, the German one, in Part One of the drama. The Grecian beauties here know Mephisto for what he is: they have seen every nymph he catches turn into a broomstick or a lizard or some other revolting symbol of his Gothic magic. The only figures in this landscape who find

Mephisto congenial are the Phorcyads, that grey threesome 'far worse than the hags of hell' who share a single eye.

Meanwhile I, guiding my glass bubble, have tracked down Thales and Anaxagoras (my examination on the pre-Socratics was yesterday), and I plead with those experts on the origin of the world to bring me to a proper birth. But Anaxagoras, with the cranes flying overhead and the earth trembling beneath his feet, falls down in fear, while Thales, in the strange way of dreams, insists that the earthquake we have just experienced hasn't happened at all. (Anaxagoras, I recall, thought life was produced by volcanic fire. Thales knew better.)

Thales takes over my quest for human birth. He leads me, flashing along in my test tube, to the 'rocky inlets of the Aegean Sea.' He knows that the life I want must begin, as everything begins, with water. But the sea god Nereus can't help me; he's little more than a crusty old crank. Luckily, Proteus (who I recall was once sought out by Menelaus, lurking under a sealskin) is attracted by the flashing of my lantern. He materializes, first as a giant tortoise and then – master of metamorphosis that he is – as a friendly dolphin. So, amid nymphs and Nereids and Sirens I ride dolphin-back by moonlight to meet the loveliest of all the ladies of the sea, Galatea. As I speed joyfully onward, Proteus – the wise old man who, when tamed, tells a hero what he needs to know – tells me what I must know, and what Faust himself eventually comes to know in his quest: I must never reach a point where I can rest. (And I thought that when this year's dozen examinations in Classics were over I could loll on my laurels!)

The dream races to its climax: across the waters, I can see Galatea on a throne of seashells. She has a mother's face, for it is she who will give me birth. Thales thrills to see life about to be re-created. I am amazed, as I speed forward, that my light shines so airily in the waves. Then suddenly I crash on Galatea's rocky inlet. The elements of earth, air, fire, and water explode around me, and I wake up.

In the literature I know, there is no passage quite so dazzling, so allusive, and – I must say, even though I haven't traced the scientific references in it – so vibrant with the science of its day as that quest of the hermaphrodite in the bubble for life's fulfilment. And in saying that I haven't forgotten the science-fiction voyage that climaxes with the birth of the Star-Child at the end of Stanley Kubrick's *2001: A Space Odyssey*.

What sort of man could have written those pages? Only, I think, one whose life was one of endless experiment, of immense creativity, of exuberant literacy, of insatiable questing for knowledge. The writings of Johann Wolfgang von Goethe fill one hundred and thirty-three volumes in the Weimar edition. The composition of *Faust* extended across sixty of his eighty-two years. Before his first version (the so-called *Urfaust* discovered a half-century after his death[3]), he had undergone a period of religious mysticism, dabbled in alchemy and occultism, studied and practised law, and written both literary essays and larger works like *Goetz von Berlichingen* (the quasi-Shakespearean flagship play of the Sturm und Drang movement) and *The Sorrows of Young Werther* (the quasi-autobiographical epistolary novel that, in its extremes of passion, prompted a wave of Romantic suicides across Europe). The imaginative experiences of Goethe's test-tube Homunculus are not unrelated to his early life.

But his life was pragmatically Faustian as well. Still in his twenties, Goethe accepted the position of minister of state from the hereditary prince of Weimar, and remained a high-ranking man of influence there for half a century, determining policy and, for many years, directing the state theatre. When he began to travel extensively, especially in Italy (writing his *Italienische Reise*), his literary interests moved from Romantic Storm and Stress to a more classical ideal, though at the same time his mind continued to range freely and enthusiastically through the sciences, and he made important contributions to mineralogy, botany, optics, and anatomy. He also wrote love poetry, for he had many loves, among them Friederike in Sesenheim (immortalized as Gretchen in *Faust*); Lotte in Wetzlar (immortalized as Charlotte in *Werther* and later, by Thomas Mann, in *Lotte in Weimar*); another Lotte in Weimar, Lotte von Stein (whose careful and almost courtly keeping Goethe at a distance inspired many of his best lyrics and prompted more than a thousand letters); the Italian girls of his *Roman Elegies* (as voluptuous as the pseudonymous mistresses of Catullus and Propertius); Marianne Willemer (immortalized as Zuleika in the *Westöstlicher Divan*); and finally Christiane Vulpius (who, in his own good time, he made his wife and the proper mother of his son).

More than that, Goethe's friendship with Friedrich Schiller, the only German of his age who was his complement and intellectual equal, resulted in a ten-year correspondence that is a literary treasure to set beside the plays (*Egmont, Iphigeneia, Tasso*), the novels (*Wilhelm Meister* and *Elective Affinities*), the hexameter narrative poem *Hermann und Dorothea*, the autobiographical *Dichtung und Wahrheit*, the hundreds of poems (many later set to music by Schubert), and above all the two parts, published a quarter-century apart, of *Faust*.

Half of Goethe's life can be set against the background of the French Revolution, which he saw as the end of the European culture he knew, and the Napoleonic Wars, in which he refused to support the claims of German nationalism. For these and other reasons he has never been without his critics, but then neither have Virgil and Wagner. Smaller minds have never forgiven him for being a bourgeois in the service of noblemen, and called him the 'poet of the business ethic.'[4] Larger minds have deplored the fact that 'in the deployment of his extra-poetic talents he often [seemed] to insist stubbornly on a playfully cultivated mediocrity.'[5] Poetasters who are sure that they can write better verses than the sixteenth-century Knittelvers that Goethe deliberately – nay, enthusiastically – sprinkled throughout his *Faust*, are, needless to say, wholly incapable of the sublimity, the pathos, the imaginative sweep of the rest of the drama's verse, which is by turns Pindaric, Euripidean, hymnic, ballad-like, delicately Alexandrine, and very often Romantically lyric. And yet, though *Faust* is a feast of metrical variety, Rainer Maria Rilke, a fine poet, said he was never able to read more than a page of it. Perhaps he could not do so because he had his own angels and demons to deal with in his quite different ways and couldn't invite Faust's into his private world. For the fact is that Goethe, in an age called enlightened, always remained aware of the darker side of human nature, and that is what most people have found fascinating about him, and what some have blamed him for unleashing in this century.

But when this century turns into the next Goethe will doubtless mean many more things. He has been called the last universal genius, favoured as he was by fate with an imposing intellect and by time by being allowed to live in the last era in which intellectuals were not expected to specialize. He was interested in, and wrote with astonishing insight about, virtually everything. But his imagination, which was as important to him as ever his reason was, was shaped to an eminent degree by the classics of Greece and Rome.

So if a mad dream is the proper way to feel one's way through that first half of Goethe's German re-creation of classic Greece, perhaps an imaginative dream of Euripidean tragedy may be the best approach to its second half – the Helen episode, which is in fact a fragment of a play Goethe had begun years before.

I have, it seems, gone back to my undergraduate sleep, and I dream now that I am in the theatre of Dionysus on the south slope of the Acropolis, watching a drama set in front of the palace of Menelaus in Sparta, on the banks of the Eurotas. A ship glides into view, and the most beautiful woman in the world steps from it. Helen of Troy has been sent ahead by Menelaus with a chorus of Trojan women to prepare a sacrifice in gratitude for their safe return from the Trojan War. I am delighted to hear, after the last dream's thousands of lines of rhymed metres of all kinds, that this woman speaks in unrhymed iambic trimeters: her delicately measured German could almost be classic Greek.

Helen makes her processional way into her husband's palace only to rush out again, for (like the priestess in Aeschylus's *Eumenides*, which I was examined on two weeks ago) she has been accosted within by a frightening old woman, who promptly emerges through the proskenion. The crone is not only fearsomely ugly but uncommonly tall, bebuskined as she is. The chorus members, one by one, engage her in an amoebean stychomythia, attempting to find out who she is. I alone know, from my first dream, that the crone is one of the Phorcyads who, sharing a single eye with her two hideous sisters, can remember everything that has ever happened. Here in front of Menelaus's palace the Phorcyad draws memories from Helen of the many men who have met their deaths because of her beauty. Helen says, 'I do not know the truth of what I am.' And all the time I note that the scene is written in Attic stasima and kommoi.

Finally the Phorcyad tells Helen that inside the temple all stands ready for the sacrifice Menelaus has ordered – all except the victim itself. *Horribile dictu*, Helen hears that *she* is the one who must fall beneath the sacrificial axe. Her husband has avoided her on the return journey because he has determined to kill her now. But there is one hope of escape. The old Phorcyad can take Helen to a fantastical castle nearby, just across Mount Taygetus, where a handsome young prince will protect her. The trumpets of Menelaus sound in the distance, and Helen makes her escape.

Mists cover the scene – and in the strange ways of dreaming I move from classic tragedy to medieval fairy tale, from chaste iambic trimeter to homely rhymed couplets. The prince in the castle, the Romantic knight in shining armour ready to defend Greek Helen is – as I ought to have suspected he would be – German Faust. Somehow, he has secured the services of that famous far-seeing Argonaut, Lynceus, to be the watchman of his tower. When Faust first sees Helen he is ready to put the faithful Lynceus to death for not properly announcing the arrival of such a famous lady. But Lynceus pleads that his lynx-eyed vision was blinded by the very sight of Helen. Then it is Faust's turn to be struck, as with an arrow, by her glance. He kneels at her feet, and he woos her by teaching her to rhyme in German couplets. When the armies of her husband are heard approaching, Faust sends his pan-German forces out to do battle, and Germany wins for Helen all of Greece.

The two lovers from different cultures then consummate their union, and the Gothic castle is transformed into a classic Arcadia. In that pastoral land where Virgil, in the fourth eclogue, once predicted the birth of a Golden-Age child, a wonderful child is now born, with the bewildering suddenness of dreams, to Helen and Faust – a child precocious as the infant Hermes, maturing by the minute, skilled at poetry, classically Greek to look upon but crazily Romantic in behaviour. Is he Virgil's Messianic *puer* or is he, as commentators never fail to point out, Goethe's fanciful figure for the Romantic poet Byron? His parents have named him Euphorion. In the dream I seem to imagine that he is I, and that I can fly.

My mother, remembering Icarus, says, 'Have a care of flying.' My father, remembering Antaeus, says, 'Remember to touch down to earth from time to time.' My dream bursts into wild song as I, suddenly grown from child to adolescent, pursue a nymph, scale the Arcadian heights with lyre in hand, leap into the air, and, as in the first dream, crash to my death.

My mother, Helen, embraces my father, Faust, and disappears into her classic myths. Faust makes his way back to Romantic Germany. And, as no dreamer ever really dies in his dreams, I find I'm once again in the theatre in Athens, facing the hideous Phorcyad, who, it now appears, has been the midwife at my birth. She picks up my fallen lyre and chiton for use by some new poet, and then removes her tragic buskins and mask to reveal herself as – Mephistopheles! Faust's personal devil has masterminded my whole dream, persuading Helen that Menelaus was going to kill her, setting Faust up in his castle, transporting Helen there for my conception and birth, and bringing all, in the end, to nothingness. Nothingness, I ought to have said earlier, is that state to which Mephistopheles tries to reduce everything in the world.

I wake up unfulfilled (there is no moment of fulfilment in dreams), but realize with relief that the final examination I shall have to contend with that day will be something infinitely less frightening than the two dreams I have had.

The world of dreams is fearful because everything there has some relation to the world we know, but seems to be kineticized, unmotivated, afloat in some irrational, unintelligible state of change. The world of dreams is, mercifully, not the world in which we live out our lives, meet our challenges, and make our conscious decisions. And yet there is a connection between the two, or at least Goethe sensed that there was. His conscious life was filled with activity. At the same time his memory and imagination were filled with, among other things, impressions he had inherited from Italy and Greece, and he knew amid the business of a busy life that this heritage was constantly working imaginatively for him. And if I have, in my dreaming, seemed impossibly solipsistic, it is as nothing compared to the self-absorption of the man who wrote *Faust*. *Faust* is a symbolic expression of Goethe's lifelong searching for experience, and perhaps of any man's search for the knowledge of himself. It is, in short, a quest.

The Faust legend was not, until Goethe, a quest at all. It was a cautionary tale, a grim warning to devout Christians not to dabble in magic as did a certain Johann (or, in some accounts, Georg) Faust who actually lived in sixteenth-century Germany. He may have been little more than a wandering mountebank, but he had an effect on a gullible public that was taken seriously by Luther and Melanchthon. And after his death the legend developed that he had sold his soul to the devil for powers and pleasures such as noman had ever known.

Some elements of the Faust story are as old as Christianity itself: in chapter 8 of the Acts of the Apostles, a certain Simon Magus tries to buy the gifts of the Holy Spirit from Saints Peter and John. This same Simon is supposed, in later legend, to have challenged Saint Peter in the presence of the emperor Nero, and to have crashed to his death in a demonstration of his power, occultly acquired, to fly. Eventually Simon was credited with the fusion of Stoicism with Gnosticism, and his consort was said to have been the embodiment of God the Father's thought. Her name, incidentally, was Helen. It hardly seems necessary to say that Goethe availed himself of some of this.

But however old and far-flung its antecedents, the Faust story has always been thought essentially German, and the product of a post-medieval age when new religious and parareligious impulses were emerging (witness the demonic elements in Brueghel and Dürer and the rise of the occult in Parcelsus), when new discoveries were being made in science (with Copernicus, Giordano Bruno, and Kepler), and when classical humanism was a new stimulus to the imagination (the conjuring up of Helen of Troy is an early and intrinsic part of the Faust story). Reactionary theologians both Protestant and Catholic who denounced these new developments had the Faust legend ready-to-hand as an example of what might happen to anyone who, in pride of intellect or craving for pleasure, attempted to overstep the bonds imposed on man by nature and the teachings of the Church.

German was the language of the earliest published version of the legend, the anonymous *Faustbuch* of 1587: the Faust we first meet in print searches through the sciences of his day in an attempt to understand the earth and the heavens, finds all knowledge inadequate, makes his pact with Mephistopheles, passes through a number of rather low erotic and magical adventures, and is dispatched to a vividly described hell when the twenty-four hours of his contract are up.

Christopher Marlowe was quick to adapt this German narrative for the English stage. In many ways, he remade it. His Doctor Faustus is damned to hellfire as Fausts before had been, but not before he has been shown to be a truly tragic figure, a man of the Renaissance who goes so far in his desire for unlimited experience, in his lust for power, in his preference (embodied in Helen of Troy) for classical learning over Sacred Scripture, that it becomes impossible for him to repent, even when he sees Christ's blood stream in the firmament.

In the century that followed Marlowe, literary versions of the Faust story appeared all over Europe. But Goethe probably came to know the legend first when he was a boy watching a puppet show, for Doctor Faust had by his time become, like Don Juan, a figure for popular entertainment: both Faust and Don Juan are heroes dispatched to hell for their sins, but only after the audience has had its fill of magic tricks and devilish pranks. Goethe was not to neglect the rude comic potential in the Faust story. But in the sixty years across which he wrote his version of it, science was gaining so much ground over traditional Christian doctrine that, to use the story at all, he had to invert it. Faust's searching for knowledge could no longer end in damnation, real or symbolic.

So it was that Goethe turned the story from cautionary tale to quest: his Faust, a modern man, would seek to find his place in a rapidly expanding world, and nature would teach him new dimensions in the received wisdom of both Christianity and classical antiquity. The new Faust would, in the face of a century or more of tradition, save himself by his endless questing. Lessing, the greatest of German literary critics, had already attempted something of this, but without success. His *Faust,* which has only partly survived (and may in fact never have been completed), was written in the full spirit of eighteenth-century optimism, and uses a truly ingenious twist: Faust is a phantom created by God to teach the devil that human learning will in the end triumph over evil. But the myth, for by now it had become much more than legend, was darker than that, and the enlightened Lessing eventually admitted that 'anyone who today would try to represent such a subject ... would be courting failure.'[6]

Goethe, in an eighteenth century fast turning into a nineteenth, began to see Faust as an image of himself – intent on understanding the secrets of nature, of the depths of the soul and the heights of the universe, driven by a love of the beautiful, by a strong erotic impulse, a questing intellect, and an awareness as well of the dangerous potential within the human soul.

He was not ashamed to show, as he wrote, the evil that mingled with the good in his own nature. When he was a young man first testing himself against the Faust myth, he was made painfully aware that he had in his ambition destroyed something beautiful, and it weighed on his conscience. Out of these feelings he introduced, for the first time in the Faust tradition, the character who would permanently change that tradition and capture the imagination of the world – the figure of Gretchen.

In his early twenties Goethe, in disguise – as was not uncommon for him on his escapades – seduced and abandoned a country parson's daughter, one Friederike Brion. She loved him 'with all her soul,' as Thomas Mann has Goethe's son (by another woman) remember.[7] But the young Goethe's ambition would not let him stay with the humble woman who gave herself to him. He said goodbye to her from his horse, shaking her hand without dismounting. Ten years later, he saw her again. She was still unwed and looked much the same. 'Here I learnt,' he said, 'what it was to be guilty.'[8]

He developed this episode of his youth, this story of innocence betrayed by a man who felt he had to experience everything in life, into Part One of *Faust*. Gretchen in Part One became the German Romantic counterpart to the classic Greek Helen of Part Two. The innocent, devout, and intense young Gretchen is, with the connivance of Mephistopheles, seduced by Faust. And that is not all. Her mother dies of the sleeping potion administered to facilitate the seduction. Her soldier brother dies defending her honour. And finally, in the madness that comes upon her when Faust abandons her, she kills their baby. When he returns, repentent, to free her with the devil's aid from her execution, she refuses to leave her prison cell, ready to die for the wrong she has done. 'Damned! (Gerichtet!)' shouts Mephistopheles. 'Saved! (Gerettet!)' announces a voice from on high. Part One of Goethe's masterpiece ends as we hear Gretchen out of total darkness call Faust by the name he had told her was his – 'Heinrich! Heinrich!' It is the most effective curtain in all of German theatre.

This, for the past century, has been the best-known part of the Faust legend, if only because it served as the basis for a French opera that, in the age of our grandparents and great-grandparents, was easily the most popular opera in all the world, the *Faust* of Charles Gounod. This wonderful piece, let it be said, is a good deal closer to Goethe's *Faust*, and especially to Goethe's early *Urfaust*, than its many critics today are willing to admit. Gounod's opera is not only full of good tunes (and the composer adroitly sees to it that the devil by no means has all the good ones), but seems as well to have captured – in the garden scene between Faust and Gretchen (called Marguerite in French), in his rapturous 'Salut' to her chaste cottage and in her enchanted 'Il m'aime' at her open window – the very spirit of romantic love. But Gretchen, or Margarethe, or Marguerite, or Margarita, has also sung to the music of Schubert and Schumann, Berlioz and Boito, Mahler and a host of lesser composers, in her 'King of Thule,' in her 'Spinning Song' ('Meine Ruh ist hin'), in her prayer to the Mater Dolorosa, in her despair at the death of her baby, in her final role as saving penitent.

So it is mainly of Goethe's first guilty love, transformed into the story of Gretchen, that we think when we open his *Faust*, and read, on the dedicatory page written late in life:

Once more you hover near me, forms and faces,
Seen long ago with troubled youthful gaze,
And shall I this time hold you, limn the traces,
Fugitive still, of those enchanted days?
You closer press: then take your powers and places,
Command me, rising from the murk and haze. (1–6)[9]

Of his 'first love' and 'life's labyrinth' Goethe says, from the vantage point of his eighties:

I feel the trembling words of song returning,
Like airs that softly on the harp-strings creep.
The stern heart softens, all its pride unlearning,
A shudder passes through me, and I weep. (27–30)

I would like, from the vantage point of that declaration, to speak at last of Goethe's spectacular revision of the main matter of the Faust tale. And though what follows is a synopsis I hope that it will also serve as something of a commentary on a drama no commentary can exhaust.

Goethe begins with a prelude in the theatre. Intent on writing a serious drama based on his own experience, he is challenged by a 'merry fellow' from that sea of faces, the audience: the play to follow must, more than anything else, entertain. He is challenged too by the theatre director: the play must have what today we would call box-office potential. Given the ingenious machinery of the nineteenth-century German stage and the ready imagination of an eager public, Goethe is encouraged to represent on the theatre's narrow boards the whole of creation's prospect 'from heaven through the world to hell.' This scene in the theatre is necessary because Goethe will, in the course of his *Faust*, mingle the serious with the comic and myth with personal experience. He will not only take us on a journey beyond the earth's confines but break virtually every rule critics ancient and modern have laid down for dramaturgy.

He will also drastically change the Faust legend, and for this we need a prologue in heaven, where the Lord sits enthroned, where primal day is saluted by three archangels, where all is vastness, clarity, and perfection, while the earth spinning below is, to the archangels, a largely unintelligible, imperfect place where light and darkness contend, where storms and tides rage majestically but senselessly.

Then the metre changes, and that fallen angel, Mephistopheles, appears to point out with mock deference that the race who live on earth would be nothing but for one gift the Lord has granted them – that 'glimmer of heaven's light' they call reason.

'Do you know my servant Faust?' asks the Lord, ready to defend his earthlings. The scene is, of course, a version of the beginning of the Book of Job.

'The Doctor?' asks the devil, implying that Faust is a fool. 'He searches for the stars of heaven and the pleasures of earth, and nothing satisfies him.'

The Lord calmly responds with the remark that reverses the whole Faust tradition: 'Though now he serves me in confusion, I shall lead him soon to clear light.'

The devil makes a wager: if he is allowed to lead Faust along *his* paths, *he* will win the learned man's soul – that is to say, Mephistopheles will satisfy Faust's passionate searching and so divert him from the creative path the Lord has set for him.

The Lord replies calmly:

> You shall have leave to do as you prefer ...
> For man must strive and striving he must err.

Of all devils, the Lord remarks, Mephisto's roguish variety (der Schalk) has never really been hated in heaven. And he adds, without Mephisto hearing, that such a devil is the devil most likely to fulfil creation's purpose in spite of himself. The Lord knows that the adventures that a spirit like Mephisto is capable of conjuring up will never provide a man like Faust with an arresting moment of complete fulfilment.

We are thus left in no suspense about the outcome of the play: the Lord will save Faust despite all his erring, for Faust will keep striving, as the creative force in the world wills him to. Though in Goethe the devil does get most of the good lines, he is in fact nothing more than the spirit that, in opposing Faust's striving, actually furthers it; in all his activity he only serves to carry out the purposes of the One who directs the creative energy in the world.

Heaven fades from view, and Mephistopheles ends the scene, as he often will in the drama to follow, with a *bon mot*, an aside to us: 'I like to see the Old Man from time to time.' But of course it is that wise 'Old Man' who has the upper hand. Goethe, while not 'of the devil's party without knowing it,' nonetheless delights in using his devil for ironic purposes. He must do so, for his Faust, the most self-absorbed of questing heroes, has little sense of the ironic, and in fact never laughs. Goethe's devil is, on the other hand, by turns insouciant, irreverent, cynical, and sardonic (when he is not having fun with Faust he turns his withering wit on university students). And there are times when we have to laugh *at* Mephisto – when, as often happens, he feels sorry for himself in his miserable work and his lack of success in it. There are also times when we fear him, for he takes his work of delaying human progress seriously. 'I am,' he declares a thousand lines into the play, 'the spirit of negation. And in this I do right, for everything that comes into existence deserves only to go out of existence. It would be better if it never existed at all. Everything you call sin, destruction, and evil is my proper element' (1.1338–44).

Strangely enough, amid all the bewildering changes of scene, and amid all of his changes of costume, this protean devil remains a static character, while Faust, though we may like him less than we like his demonic companion, strives, as the Lord said he would, dynamically. He errs ('Es irrt der Mensch, solong' er strebt'), but in striving or, to use our word, questing he does not utterly lose the way ('Ein guter Mensch in seinem dunklen Drange / Ist sich des rechten Weges wohl bewusst').

There is another superhuman force in the drama, though its importance is a subject of contention among readers of Goethe – the Earth-Spirit. When we descend to earth and first discover Faust in his book-lined study, the aged doctor is in despair that all his learning (he has studied his way through all four faculties of the medieval German university[10]) has served no good purpose. He has achieved no more, for all his studies, than has the grinning skull upon his desk. His only contribution to mankind has been to add with his nostrums more deaths to the thousands already caused by plague. He turns by lamplight from learning to magic, and conjures up, in a shining red flame, the Earth-Spirit – a frightening apparition neither good nor evil, not quite the Lord of the prologue in heaven and certainly not the Mephistopheles who wagered there with the Lord. Possibly the Earth-Spirit is the source of all the inscrutable change on earth that the three arch-angels saw from the heights.[11]

In any case, the Spirit knows all that Faust has not yet experi-enced and ardently longs to experience on earth. It could be of the greatest importance to him. It hovers briefly, speaks laconi-cally, and then, in the most sudden and surprising exit in the whole surprising drama, abandons the philosopher as soon as the philosopher claims equality with it. Though in a later scene Faust thanks the Spirit for giving him all he asked for, the Spirit never appears or speaks again. Instead, Faust hears a knock on the door and finds himself facing his spiritless laboratory assist-ant, Wagner. (Goethe's dramatic sense, like his thinking, is dia-lectical, and he often confounds the expectations of readers by interlaying serious and comic scenes.)

Then Mephistopheles introduces himself to Faust, in three different guises. On Easter morning, when Faust is intent on doing away with himself and is deterred by church bells and the songs of angels calling up memories of his childhood, his assigned devil appears to him in one of hell's most familiar medi-eval shapes – as a black dog that leaves flaming footprints. With this strange figure at his feet, Faust opens the New Tes-tament and proceeds to change it – for in the drama to follow Goethe will think and feel his way through Christianity, re-mythologizing its symbols and reordering its texts: 'In the begin-ning was the Word,' Faust reads. But that cannot be true: he has studied words on words to no avail. Better to say, 'In the begin-ning was the Thought.' But does thought strive, as he wants to do? Better to say, 'In the beginning was the Power.' That comes closer to his ambition. But in the end he changes the Bible pas-sage to read, 'In the beginning was the Deed.' So the first earthly guise of Mephistopheles prompts Faust to the realization that the essence and meaning of life is the very striving that the Lord allowed him in the prologue in heaven.

Mephistopheles next appears in Faust's study in the guise of a university scholar, posing as Faust's intellectual equal so as to acquaint him with the dialectic that will mark his striving. In answer to Faust's question 'Who are you?' Mephisto replies,

> Part of a power that would
> Alone work evil, but engenders good ...
> Part of a part am I, that once was all. (1335–6; 1349)

Amazingly, Mephistopheles, an angel fallen from the service of the Lord, actually knows that he does the work of the Lord even as he opposes it. He knows that his every attempt to bring everything to nothing will only strengthen and further the evolutionary design of the Lord. He is the counterforce to a force that will only grow stronger by the opposition he presents to it. Yet even with this awareness he must remain true to his nature: he must attempt to destroy the creative action of the Lord. Faust is fascinated, and the devil leaves him lulled to sleep by dreams that render the old doctor vulnerable to his influence.

Mephistopheles makes his third appearance as a squire to the questing knight Faust will be, with brocade on his coat, a feathered cap on his head, an impudent blade at his side. Faust is anxious to test with his companion the experiences he has been promised. As in the old tradition, the compact between them is written in blood. But it is a compact new with Goethe: Mephisto must provide for Faust one moment so arresting that it will halt his onward quest for experience. Faust's soul will be Mephisto's if Mephisto can bring Faust to an experience so fulfilling that he will choose to remain in it and say 'Verweile doch, du bist so schön':

> If to the fleeting hour I say
> 'Remain, so fair thou art, remain!'
> Then bind me with your fatal chain,
> For I will perish in that day. (1699–1702)

As Faust has already cursed all that can fulfil him – honour, family, pride, money, faith, hope, love, and, most of all, patience – it seems that Mephistopheles might now have a hard time of it. And he does.

Two preparatory adventures follow: the encounter with the university students in Auerbach's Cellar in Leipzig (a place where, I was delighted on my own travels to discover, you can still find as much lively fun among the students as Faust does in the pages of Goethe), and a Witch's Kitchen (a place I never found in my travels, else I might have had a glimpse of Helen of Troy and been transformed, as Faust is till his last adventure, to a man thirty years of age).

Then the questing starts. Mephistopheles is clever, but he is not clever enough to know that he can never arrest Faust by appealing, as he invariably does, to his lower instincts. Mephisto is sure that sex is his strongest suit. After the misadventure with Gretchen – with much too much guilt among the exaltation for it ever to be the experience to end Faust's striving – Mephistopheles attempts to distract Faust with a German Walpurgisnacht. This abandoned, brimstony affair, largely written in the doggerel that has offended some (surely it is Goethe's way of satirizing critics and personal enemies) only leaves Faust lamenting that the Earth-Spirit has given him so vulgar a devil as Mephistopheles to be his companion. When, in the midst of the revels he sees a vision of Gretchen, sentenced to death for the murder of her child, he hurries to her prison cell to save her, fails to do so, and is haunted by her cry 'Heinrich! Heinrich!' from the darkness.

As the Lord predicted would happen, Faust has erred in his striving. Error is, as we have seen before, a consequence of questing. 'Only the contemplative man,' a leading Goethian rightly observes, 'can keep his soul pure. This is the inescapable contradiction imposed upon human existence.'[12]

Faust needs to be rehabilitated after his seduction of Gretchen, as Goethe had to be after his first betrayal. The opening scene in Part II, written years later, is one of the most beautiful things he ever wrote. In the pure air of an Alpine glen, nature and life and the desire to strive toward good take possession of Faust. He finds new purpose in the *terza rima* of Dante and Calderón, amid burgeoning and quivering boughs. An erring, unworthy man, he cannot look into the sun as it rises (it is, perhaps, an image of the complete truth he searches for), but he can continue his quest in the sunlight refracted by nature's cleansing waters into the many-coloured rainbow:

> And so I turn, the sun upon my shoulders,
> To watch the water-fall, with heart elate,
> The cataract pouring, crashing from the boulders,
> Split and rejoined a thousand times in spate:
> The thundrous water seethes in fleecy spume,
> Lifted on high in many a flying plume,
> Above the spray-drenched air. And then how splendid
> To see the rainbow rising from this rage,
> Now clear, now dimmed, in cool sweet vapour blended.
> So strive the figures on our mortal stage.
> This ponder well, the mystery closer seeing;
> In mirrored hues we have our life and being. (4715–27)

But Faust's return to the world of mirrored hues is only a new kind of failure. Part Two continues with scenes of skulduggery at the court of the financially and spiritually bankrupt Holy Roman Empire, with Mephistopheles disguised as the jester. It is sumptuous entertainment and social satire provided by a poet who, as a long-time public servant, was all too well acquainted with money-making, end-justifies-the-means politics. 'Who needs such concepts as Nature and Mind,' seems to be his ironic question, 'when in the real world all is controlled by Church and State?'

The 'real world' we see is a sham, a carnival court in which the ladies masquerade as olive branches and golden ears of corn, where mere entertainers presume to sing the songs of the three Graces and the three Fates, where Prudence rides on an elephant, where the Emperor appears as Pan, singeing his beard in his lust for gold, and where Faust, with Poetry as his boy charioteer, appears as Plutus blithely dispensing money to the crowds – for with the aid of Mephisto he has devised a flimsy plan for keeping all this decadence afloat.

It is in this worldly milieu that Goethe's Faust conjures up his vision of Helen of Troy. This is not the Helen episode we detailed earlier in this chapter but the obligatory raising of the phantom Helen, as old as the Faust tradition itself. And of all the carnival scenes, it bears most on the concerns of these chapters, for it is here that Goethe deals most explicitly with some of the archetypes we have found in our other quests. If Mephistopheles is the hero's shadow (and there is hardly a more clearly delineated Jungian shadow), he must have a connection with the feminine. Mephistopheles tells Faust that, to conjure up Helen, he must descend to what he calls 'the Mothers.'

'The Mothers!' Faust exclaims with a shudder, as if he has heard a voice from a collective unconscious.[13] To find these timeless figures one must travel beneath the earth to an eternal void. Mephistopheles decribes the journey, for he knows Nothingness well: if you were to swim to the immensity that is ocean's end, you would still see *something* – the waves that with each passing moment take form and then change again; but in the journey to the Mothers you arrive at the very source of forming and changing again. You see Nothing. Faust tells Mephisto he is determined to make the quest: 'For in your Nothing I hope to find the All.'

Mephistopheles provides Faust with a key that, like the talismans of other quests, glows in his hand. Neither we nor Mephistopheles, whom we might have expected to serve as sibylline guide, make the descent along with the hero. Faust journeys alone, and the quest is described only in advance by his devil: in the depth of depths, which might as easily be the height of heights, Faust will see, by the glow of a burning tripod, the Mothers –

Formation, Transformation,
Eternal Mind's eternal recreation. (6827–8)

Faust will see the sources of perpetual change. He will see, perhaps, a mutable chaos that Plato, with his immutable ideas, never knew, or the anima-depths of his own creative soul, or the mind of God where, in medieval thought, ideas were born. The danger is great, but Faust will be safe if he touches the burning tripod with the key. The symbols are almost endlessly suggestive.

Faust sinks, with the key in his hand, beneath the earth, and re-emerges at the imperial court two scenes later with the key, the tripod, and, soon thereafter, a vision of Helen. But neither the key, glowing in his hand, nor an invocation of the Mothers themselves, can win Helen for him. She appears before the court making love to another man – Paris – and, a form without substance, she vanishes when Faust tries to embrace her.

The scene is another Faustian experiment gone wrong. But beneath the earth the hero has glimpsed, in mysterious symbols, something of the reality lying within himself in ever-changing feminine form. This is a preliminary hint, however dim, of the drama's eventual and very surprising resolution.

But before that final resolution we witness Faust's greatest failure, his most hybristic deed.[14] After corrupting the Holy Roman Empire for his own ends, Faust attempts to dominate nature, which till now has filled him with awe and restored him after his failures. He attempts in fact to dominate that motherly element in nature that is most endless, formless, and changing – water.

Faust has, in the drama's final act, built himself a magnificent seaport and pleasure palace, to which Mephistopheles has brought, by commerce or by piracy, the wealth of the world. At eighty years of age – Goethe's own age as he writes – Faust makes it his ultimate ambition to control the sea. In this he is not entirely megalomaniacal: he hopes to harvest what Homer called the unharvested sea for the good of humankind, to build for man a paradise on earth.

For this end he might have used his soul's potential – the creative energy that he has glimpsed deep within himself. But, encouraged by his personal devil, the increasingly sinister Mephistopheles, he resorts instead to magic arts. More and more his experiences have become those of a man who seeks, in Erich Heller's phrase, 'power over life through actions that overreach the reaches of his soul.'[15] Heller suggests, and I am sure he is right, that the black magic Faust now uses is Goethe's symbol for activity that, in rejecting human potential, destroys human feeling.

In a single night the sea is tamed by shrieking demons working with floods of fire. The once unproductive waters yield vast stretches of dry land, green fields in which civilization can flourish. But Faust can take no pleasure in his achievement. As great ships sail peacefully into port, he is maddened by the silver sound of a chapel bell. The keepers of the chapel are Philemon and Baucis, two pious figures Goethe has borrowed from Book 8 of Ovid's *Metamorphoses*. They are an old couple who have, through all the days when the sea was dangerous, saved travellers with the sound of their bell. Now that the sea has receded, they and their cottage beneath the linden trees and their chapel with its silvery sound of warning are not needed any more – though even now a mysterious Wayfarer whose life they once saved has returned after many years to bless them. (If Ovid's *Metamorphosis* is intended as a parallel, this Wayfarer at the cottage of Philemon and Baucis might be the Lord of Goethe's prologue, or one of his angels, in disguise.)

Faust hates the chaste cottage, 'not just because it is a hindrance to his engineering plans, but because it is a reminder of his first great guilt'[16] in seducing Gretchen. He hates the sound of the bell because it reminds him of the church bells that long ago prevented his taking his own life. He hates the pious pair because they acknowledge the old God 'who had permitted the sea to rage' and not him, the beneficent new god who has 'replaced that raging sea with ... "an image of paradise."'[17]

Intent on driving the old man and woman off the land that he and he alone has made safe for civilization, Faust blindly commands Mephistopheles to dispossess them. Some nineteenth-century commentators, seeing *Faust* as a drama in which man eventually saves himself by making the world a better place, have attempted to justify this action.[18] But clear-eyed Lynceus, surveying the beauty of the landscape and speaking from his watchtower one of Goethe's loveliest lyrics, weeps as he sees the cottage set afire and the old couple consumed by flames. Mephistopheles returns to say that he and his minions have had to kill the Wayfarer too.

The deaths of these innocents do not go unavenged. Faust is visited by four Furies, and the last of them, Sorge (Anxiety), strikes him blind. In his megalomania, all of his good qualities – love of nature, constant striving, hope for improving the world – have led only to destruction. Not one of his adventures has been, from any moral point of view, anything better than ambivalent. And yet, when he is blinded, he says, not unlike Milton's blinded Samson, that with darkness now all around him 'a light shines clear' within him.

In the scenes that follow, Goethe confided to his amanuensis Johann Peter Eckermann, Faust is 'precisely one hundred years old.'[19] It is time at last for him to lose or to save his soul – that is to say, in our terms, which I hope are at least partly Goethe's – to fail or succeed in his quest to find himself. Sightless, groping his way like Oedipus, he leaves his palace, rejoicing in what he thinks is the sound of further work to reclaim land from the sea on behalf of mankind. But what he hears is in reality the sound of the demon spades digging his grave. He speaks to his overseer, not knowing that his overseer is Mephistopheles:

> Ay, in this thought I pledge my faith unswerving,
> Here wisdom speaks its final word and true,
> None is of freedom or of life deserving
> Unless he daily conquers it anew. (11573–6)

A century old, Faust is still ready to start his life anew. And his thought is not, finally, of using black magic, a dubious source from without, but of finding within himself the reserves to make his life a life of purpose. He hopes still, despite his failures, to benefit mankind, to see 'Standing on freedom's soil, a people free.' At the point of death, when Mephistopheles has the grave ready for him, Faust says of that hope for the future:

> Then to the moment could I say:
> Linger you now, you are so fair! (11581–2)

He speaks the very 'Verweile doch, du bist so schön' that was to lose his soul for him. But Mephistopheles has not noticed, as his demons lay the dead man on the sand, that Faust has not reached the moment to end his questing, but only come to a vision of it.

Mephistopheles, an unacademic sort, is not ready to grant it to grammar that, in introducing the fateful line, Faust has used a subjunctive (dürft' ich), and has not said the fateful line unconditionally. In fact, Faust cannot, being Faust, ever say the line – for it would mean an end to his striving. The Lord knew that from the beginning.

Mephistopheles, poised with his attendants to snatch that 'fluttering, fleeting thing,' Faust's soul, as it leaves the body, is unable to do so. Angels descend, scattering roses that burn like brimstone when they touch the devils. Goethe, like the greatest artists, introduces comic touches at his peak moments: the prudish Mephistopheles, already smarting under the strewn roses, is driven to distraction by the rosy behinds of heaven's cherubs. And it is at that moment, when the devil is embarrassed as never before, that the angels rescue Faust's immortal part and take it to heaven.

Faust's striving has, in a scene in which the tongue-in-cheek boldness of the author has confounded many interpreters, saved him. But how, Goethe wondered (and later confessed to Eckermann that he wondered[20]) could he represent the final redemption of a hero who had, in all previous versions of his myth, been damned? Goethe probably remembered a fresco he had seen in the Campo Santo at Pisa: hermits emerging from their mountain caves in wonder as flights of angels soar upwards towards the Virgin Mary. In Goethe's last pages, his hero, reborn like a chrysalis and accompanied by a choir of baby boys who died at birth, rises upwards on his final quest. He journeys aloft past a series of Wise Old Men: Pater Ecstaticus, pierced through with love's arrows; Pater Profundus, surveying all of nature from depth to height; Pater Seraphicus, sustained by the Beatific Vision and wafting into its presence the innocent children who never lived their lives to completion.

But it is not the wisest of old men, the Lord of Goethe's prologue, who is the summit of Faust's journey. From the highest, purest mountain cliff, we hear the voice of the male figure who heralds the appearance of the female. He is Doctor Marianus, rapt by a vision of the Virgin Mary. That most loving archetype of the feminine stands on high, bestowing forgiveness on those who come penitent to her feet. Mary Magdalen is kneeling there, as are the Samaritan Woman who spoke with Jesus at the well and, from the Acts of the Apostles, Maria Aegyptiaca. Then, coming clearer in the vision, is someone who is first identified only as Una Poenitentium and then as 'she who was called Gretchen.' The words she once prayed in need to the Mater Dolorosa:

Neige
Du Schmerzenreiche
Dein Antlitz gnädig meiner Not! (3588–90)

she prays now in joy to the Mater Gloriosa:

Neige, neige,
Du Ohnegleiche,
Du Strahlenreiche
Dein Antlitz meinem Glück! (12069–72)

Faust draws near in the beauty of his youthful body and, though the circling angels have sung that he has learned much and has much to teach them, the penitent once called Gretchen asks that he may learn from her, and be guided by her through these new regions. The Virgin Mary nods assent, and Faust is led onwards by the one he had once loved and left.

We cannot, of course, interpret these very Catholic images strictly according to any theology. Neither, as the Protestant theologian Jaroslav Pelikan says, can we entirely dismiss their symbolic aspects.[21] The drama ends as it began, in a literary heaven: the opening prologue draws on the Book of Job and the closing scene calls Dante to mind (at the height of heaven, Dante does not look directly at God, but sees Him through the Beatrice that has led him onwards). Goethe's deliberate balancing reinforces the questing idea in his new version of the Faust myth: his prologue assures us that the hero will strive, and err so long as he strives, and yet be guided to salvation, while his last scene affirms that his hero has indeed been saved in spite of his erring, because of his striving. More than that, the final scene suggests that life beyond the life we know is, like the life we know, a quest, an upwardly spiralling process of ever knowing more, learning more, loving more.

There has not, till now, been much of love in Goethe's poem. But the source of his hero's striving, we hear with some surprise in the drama's last song, has been the feminine within him:

> Alles Vergängliche
> Ist nur ein Gleichnis;
> Das Unzulängliche,
> Hier wird's Ereignis;
> Das Unbeschreibliche,
> Hier ist's Getan;
> Das Ewig-Weibliche
> Zieht uns hinan. (12104–11)

> Everything that has happened is only a parable.
> What is insufficient is here fulfilled.
> What is indescribable comes here to pass.
> The Eternal Feminine leads us onwards.

What is this Eternal Feminine, this force that has drawn the hero upwards and saved him? Some would say that it is Faust's own love of and reverence for nature (in dem Allverein / Selig zu sein, 11807–8). Others, that it is his unfulfilled yearning for the Helen of his imagination and the Gretchen of his youthful passion. Still others, that it is the hero's fidelity to the Mothers – to the creative feminine within him as opposed to the inhuman knowledge symbolized in the drama by magical arts. But it is wrong, or at best a partial view, to limit 'das Ewig-Weibliche' solely to a force operating within the hero. There has been much self-initiated striving in the drama, but there has also, we are now told, been a saving action above and beyond the self that has contributed to its saving, and Goethe does not hesitate to call it love, and to make it clear that it is the love that a power beyond Faust feels for him. The angels who bear Faust's immortal part upwards proclaim: 'This man who now shares our spirit world is saved from evil. For we can save the man who ever strives and toils. And if the love that comes from on high has taken his part as well, the host of the blessed will give him greeting from the heart.'

In the last year of his life Goethe said, in conversation with Eckermann, 'These verses contain the key to Faust's redemption: in Faust himself an ever higher and purer activity right to the end, and from above the eternal love that comes to his aid.'[22] Faust is saved by his striving *and* by what Goethe's angels call 'the love that comes from on high.' This combination of human striving and divine aid is, to the dismay of some commentators, uncomfortably close to the Christian doctrine of faith and good works. Goethe himself went on in his conversation with Eckermann to say, 'This is quite in harmony with our religious ideas, according to which we are saved not by our own powers alone, but through the supervening divine grace.'[23] The end of a man's personal quest is – in Goethe as in Homer, Virgil, and Wagner – a matter of his facing archetypes within himself *and* of cooperating with more than human forces beyond himself.

There can be no one explanation of Goethe's *Faust*. Some four years earlier, its author had also said, 'That the devil loses the wager and that a man forever striving upwards from grave aberrations to what is better can be *saved* is indeed a good, efficacious thought which explains much, but it is not an *idea* that underlies the whole work and each individual scene.'[24] It is Goethe's dismissal of any one 'idea' explaining his *Faust* that encouraged me to begin this discussion with an evocation, via an undergraduate's dream, of the most riotous of the drama's symbolic scenes. For *Faust* is in the end a work of the imagination for the imagination. It is not a text from which ideas can be extracted. It is science, religion, art, and life transformed, in scene after scene, into poetic vision.[25] Its meaning lies not in ideas but in the relationships we establish, reading and wondering, among its many symbols. It is a poem written by a man preoccupied with the scientific analysis of plants, animals, and colours. It is written, appropriately for a work whose origins lay in experimenting with magic, as a series of transformations. Of all the surviving literature of Greece and Rome, the work it most resembles is Ovid's

Metamorphoses, and especially that scene in Book 7 where Medea, flying over Ovid's world, sees everything below as a series of endless transformations.

Goethe's Faust makes his way, not through the ordered world of the Middle Ages (where man cannot overstep his bounds without sinning), and not through the self-confident world of the Renaissance (where man is fixed at the centre of experience), but through the era bridging the eighteenth and nineteenth centuries (where man must find his place in a world that is rapidly and relentlessly changing). Faust's life becomes, accordingly, a quest. In questing, he undergoes as many transformations as does the devil who accompanies him, as many as does the world through which he moves. Everything that is possible for man has to be experienced by Faust before he can think of himself as, in the terms of the prologue and final scene, saved.

Goethe's drama is not seen in its full dimension until one has noticed the metamorphoric element in it. Faust the ambivalent quester is figured in those fantastic seekers for new life, Homunculus and Euphorion. Mephistopheles materializes in each of three early scenes in a different guise, and later assumes the appearances of jester, Phorcyad, and chief engineer building against the sea. The Eternal Feminine appears in the archetypal Mothers and also in Gretchen, Galatea, Helen, and the Virgin Mary (all of whom, in quite different ways in quite different scenes, are mothers). Even something of the Lord himself may be thought to reappear as the Earth-Spirit, as Proteus in the Classical Walpurgisnacht, as the Wayfarer received by Philemon and Baucis. In Jungian terms each of these figures – persona, shadow-side, anima, and Wise Old Man – is an aspect of Faust's soul, the upwardly-spiralling saving of which (that is to say, the mandala-integration of its conflicting aspects, its impulses, its dark forces, its ambitions) is the theme of this quest as much as it has been of the others we have considered.

The contradictions in Faust are the contradictions in Goethe himself. He was a sceptic who believed in God, a reasoning man who kept in close contact with his unreasoning psyche, a seeker of scientific knowledge who nonetheless stood in awe before the mysteries of nature and the cosmos. He would not, and probably could not, build a system out of his studies. Systems were for Kant. Goethe, though he never stopped putting his reason to work, knew that reason could never comprehend and order all things, least of all the many-dimensioned thing that was himself.

When Erich Heller said that Goethe's hero came to represent 'a whole epoch in history, its lust for knowledge, for power over nature, its intellectual and emotional insatiability, its terrible failure in love, humility and patience,'[26] he meant the whole epoch we have called Western civilization. But of course Faust is mainly Germany's myth, and when Germany, in the years leading to the Second World War, reordered itself into a dehumanized socialist state, Albert Schweitzer cried out, 'What ... can this mean except that we, like Faust, have erred terribly in detaching ourselves from nature and surrendering ourselves to the unnatural?' And to that he added, prophetically, 'What is now taking place in this terrible epoch of ours except a gigantic repetition of the drama of Faust on the stage of the world? The cottage of Philemon and Baucis burns with a thousand tongues of flame!'[27] It was said after the war that Goethe's *Faust*, with its semiblasphemous 'in the beginning was the Deed,' with its licensing of the exceptional man to pass beyond the limits of experience, was a dangerous work, threatening in its implications, as open to misinterpretation as Nietzsche's Übermensch. Germany's Faustian soul as Spengler had seen it – an intelligence passionately embarked on the conquest of limitless space – was thought, after the Nazi era, to be something to be tamed, if not destroyed. It was not for nothing that Goethe had subtitled his *Faust* 'eine Tragödie': the old Faust figure, who had been damned because he dared to pass beyond the natural state of man, became in Goethe truly tragic, more than tragic, because his endless striving prompted him to commit endless crimes. For a time the work that had been thought the masterpiece of German literature became almost a source of shame to Germans. Buchenwald lay only a short distance from the heart of Weimar. With the Second World War, Karl Jaspers said, 'We came face to face with experiences in which we had no inclination to read Goethe, but took up Shakespeare, or the Bible, or Aeschylus, if it was possible to read at all.'[28]

But Goethe is more than the first half of our century has made of him. His hero knows all too well that 'two souls' dwell within his breast – the one prone to earthly ambitions and desires, the other aspiring ever to higher states of awareness. Faustian striving accomplished in post-war West Germany a *Wirtschaftswunder* and shaped a pacifist, democratic nation that a new generation could take pride in. At the century's end Goethe's *Faust* seems once more to be saying that the impulse 'to strive, to seek, to find, and not to yield' is good, and should be trusted. In following it a man can be, however we choose to interpret the prelude's Christian terms, the 'servant' of the Lord.

Like all classics, *Faust* speaks anew to every age. Today it is most often read as the symbolically autobiographical work of a man who devoted himself to the potential within him and strove to expand human knowledge in a hundred ways. New readers respond to its call to understand oneself and to find one's place in a changing world. But ultimately it is as a work of art that *Faust* speaks best to the future. It is more than modern, still awaiting the attention of artists who will learn from its daring mixture of sounds and symbols from different eras, its dreamlike suspension of cause and effect, its pre-Wagnerian exploration of the psyche, its sometimes Virgilian pathos, and its danger-fraught but essentially optimistic and so almost Homeric questing.

CHAPTER SIX

What Ithacas Mean

In the fifth chapter of *Don Quixote*, the parish priest and the village barber sentence the old quester's knight-errant books to be burned. They hope thereby to cure the madness that made the would-be hero an anomaly in his own time and place. Even those extreme measures are not enough for Don Quixote's niece and housekeeper. They want *all* the books in his library destroyed, 'for they have sent to perdition the finest mind in all La Mancha.'

Then as we turn Cervantes's page we discover that the barber and the priest are themselves not immune to the pleasures to be found in stories of questing, and in the end they find it in their hearts to spare some of the old man's library. While dozens of dangerous volumes are subject to inquisitorial inspection and then unceremoniously tossed out the window to await immolation in the yard below, the barber defends, among the books of chivalric romance, *Amadís de Gaula* as the first such piece to appear in Spain and so deserving of clemency. The priest is inclined to spare the old man's extensive collection of pastoral literature (among them Cervantes's own *La Galatea*). But the insistent niece pleads against the pastoral works as well: 'Ah, but Señor! Your Grace should send them to be burned along with the rest; for I shouldn't wonder at all if my uncle, after he has been cured of this chivalry sickness, reading one of these books, should take it into his head to become a shepherd and go wandering through the woods and meadows singing and piping, or, what is worse, become a poet, which they say is an incurable disease and one that is very catching.'[1]

In the seventeeth century the pastoral romance had in fact spread from Italy to Spain and was beginning to replace in popularity the romance of the questing knight. Yet the tradition in which the wandering hero battled beasts, giants, magicians and whole armies to right wrongs and to prove his devotion to the beautiful woman he loved from afar was not to die out completely. Such knights may never have existed (and certainly never existed as depicted in the romances), but the ideals of bravery, courtesy, constancy, and *noblesse oblige* exemplified in the ideal of chivalry, and in chivalry's images and symbols, continued to shape the mores of aristocratic Europe for centuries.[2]

I have thought it appropriate to begin this ending with another paragraph or two from the book that is supposed to have ended the quest tradition, for I have often felt that *Don Quixote* did not so much mark the end of that tradition as cleanse it of false elements and enable it to flourish anew, in such works as *Faust* and *Parsifal*. Certainly Cervantes's book is much more than an extended satire on the old romances of chivalry. But readers who feel initially that it may be an attack on royalty, or the church, or the Spanish society of Cervantes's day, or else that it is, like Chrétien's epic centuries before, some sort of mystical allegory, will not find much critical support for their views, and eventually they will abandon them as they begin to realize, quite rightly, that in reading *Don Quixote* they are reading about their poor selves. The bone-thin idealist quester and his big-bellied realist squire are figures to personify, as Coleridge said on several occasions,[3] the two elements of human nature – soul and sense. For a more recent writer they are soul and sense in search of something greater than themselves:

The fate of Don Quixote may *suggest* to some people the idea that knight-errantry was an absurd fancy of a deranged mind; in fact it means something totally different; it is an expression in a deliberately grotesque form of something very real, and true, and profound – of the idea that greatness lies in the urge to look for greatness, and the real butt of the satire is not Don Quixote, but the people around him who think that by burning his books they can destroy what these books had taught him – and us all.[4]

It would have been difficult to consider *Don Quixote* with the four questing works that, I hope, have taught us all, for *Don Quixote*, to achieve its ends, inverts the perspectives of the other works, turning the heroic to the commonplace, the vision to illusion, the poetry to prose. But it nonetheless confirms through its own perspective what we have found in the works that have been our main concern – that the quest is our own journey of self-discovery.

What ought we to say, finally, as we juxtapose our four heroes? First, that none of them is by any means perfect. We anticipated from the start that all of them would fail at some point in their searching, and they have: Odysseus, in the first incident of his homeward journey, sacks a city, kills its men, and enslaves its women and children; Aeneas falls several times from *pietas* into *furor*; Parsifal fails at first in the understanding and compassion that will be his fulfilment, and Faust, a great sinner, is guilty of betrayal, fraud, megalomania, and, at least indirectly, murder. The goodness of these heroes, like their greatness, lies in their struggling onwards despite their errors to find in themselves that which will enable them to transcend their failings and become the men they are called, by a power that lies beyond them, to be.

Secondly, they suffer in their searching. This, as writers on myths of many ages observe, is the lot of questing heroes:

The desert, wilderness, wasteland – the valley of the shadow of death – must be endured; the impassable rivers and seas must be safely forded. The hero is cast into the pit, abyss, chasm, cavern, ark, and tomb. But only in order to transcend them, reborn, redeemed. There are the numberless tenuous bridges to be crossed; the endless succession of ladders to ascend and descend; the clashing rocks and active doors between which we must pass with lightning speed. There are the floating islands to be transformed into firm ground, the twisted paths to be straightened, the ways that are closed to be opened, the darkness to be made light.[5]

Thirdly, what they find, in an outward symbol of wholeness, is the inner self, what it is that they truly are. Our four heroes exclaim, in effect, 'It is *my* bed and mine alone.' 'It is the bough revealed to me by *my* mother to lead me to *my* father.' 'It is the Grail *I* saw and rescued and restored to wholeness when I felt the world's pain in *myself*.' 'It is *my* eternal feminine, the one permanent thing within me that led me through all the becoming and changing phenomena of the world.' Each hero has found the meaning of his life, his struggles, his *agon*, his questing in what, fundamentally, he is and he alone. Each can be said truly to have lived the life given him.

Finally, and most important, all four heroes may be thought to be figures for us who read or listen to their adventures. Perhaps only two of them may be thought figures for the artists who give us their stories: the heroes of Wagner and Goethe are to a degree the intuitive, self-absorbed, endlessly productive geniuses who fashioned them. But we know too little about the author of the *Odyssey* to say anything about him in this regard. And with Virgil the mythic journey, which reaches a climax but not a conclusion, is the journey not of the poet but of his patron, Caesar Augustus, still in mid-career and faced with a moment of moral decision.

But if we cannot find all four of our artists in the heroes they have made, we can nonetheless find ourselves there, for the artists, in telling their tales, have wisely availed themselves of the mythic images that Gerald Vann has called 'the heritage of humanity,'[6] and Kerényi and Eliade the images through which 'the world speaks,'[7] and Jung the archetypes of a collective unconscious – images in the depths of the memory of us all.

One truth our century has discovered, or rather rediscovered, is that mythologies have in past ages supplied the symbols that give meaning to life. We have discovered that symbols are important to, indeed the very stuff of, the psyche, and that symbolic thinking is at least as important to humankind as is rational thought. Science has in our lifetime clearly benefited mankind in many ways, not least of which is the focusing of intellect on the pursuit of objective truth. But myth and symbol have their uses unknown to science. They preserve the sense, valuable to all humans, of ambivalence, mystery, religion, and poetry. Symbolic thinking is, as Eliade tells us, consubstantial with the human being, preceding language and discursive reasoning. The symbol reveals certain aspects of reality – the deepest aspects – which defy all other modes of knowledge. Images, symbols, and myths are not irresponsible creations of the psyche: they meet a need and fulfil a function, to unveil the most secret modalities of being ... If the mind makes use of images to grasp the ultimate reality of things this is precisely because that reality manifests itself in a contradictory fashion and so cannot be expressed in concepts ... To have imagination is to see the world in its totality, for it is images that have the power and function of showing forth all that eludes conceptual thinking.[8]

There is a healing power, an element of the sacred, a half-acknowledged religious reality in archetypal works of art that we cannot do without. For the theologian Gerald Vann the symbolism of the hero's journey, also found in the Bible and Christian ritual,

becomes thrilling for us because, being the universal life-pattern, it reveals itself to me as the pattern of – and the clue to – my life, my struggles, my *agon*, my joys and sorrows, my problems, my distresses, my quest for God, my glimpses of God, my journey to God. But then there is the further thrill of finding the same pattern repeated everywhere ... the pattern of the quest for life through death, endlessly stated and restated in the world's art and literature and story and fantasy and dream.[9]

The quest is the myth each of us is called to live. A Greek poet of our time has intimated this:

> When you start on your journey to Ithaca,
> then pray that the road is long,
> full of adventure, full of knowledge ...
> Always keep Ithaca fixed in your mind.
> To arrive there is your ultimate goal ...
> And if you find her poor, Ithaca has not defrauded you.
> With the great wisdom you have gained, with so much experience,
> you must surely have understood by then what Ithacas mean.'[10]

The quest you read about or listen to and wonder about is your own quest to discover yourself.

But what about that old debunker Don Quixote, who refuses in the end to acknowledge that his questing was an expression of his real self at all, who disowns his adventures as he lies dying? Ostensibly, Cervantes at the end of his greatest work returns to his initial purpose – to defeat a moribund and by his day spurious tradition, and presumably to defeat as well the myth that it preserved. I say ostensibly and presumably, because Cervantes's ending, which chimes with his beginning, is conditioned by so much journeying in between that, while we may be grateful that a false and clichéd tradition of knight-errancy has been defeated, we cannot reject the ideal of the quest itself. Some form of it is essential to our existence, and no moment in *Don Quixote* is more touching than Sancho's pleading through his tears on the last page, 'Ah, master, don't die ... Get up from this bed and let us go out into the fields clad as shepherds as we agreed to do. Who knows but behind some bush we may come upon the lady Dulcinea ... He who is vanquished today will be the victor tomorrow.' Sancho, the realist who in the first chapters has serious doubts about his idealist master, comes gradually to accept the questing ideal, to believe it and to want to live it. Though he is not Don Quixote, Don Quixote's quest, he realizes, corresponds to something within him that is necessary to him – and to his master.

When some of the old hidalgo's books were spared the flames, his housekeeper ran to fetch a basin of holy water and a branch of hyssop for the priest, with the plea that he sprinkle the spared books well, lest one of the remaining enchanters speak from the shelves and bewitch them all. The four enchanters we have dealt with may approach questing in four different ways – through oral epic, written epic, music drama, poetic drama – but each of them speaks with a power that no one has been able to exorcize, and I hope that in speaking about them we have seen something of the wonder of ourselves. Our purpose in life, they say, is not mere survival, not simply to propagate, to build and to die, but to become, with help from beyond ourselves, truly human. In psychological terms, that means integration and wholeness. In traditional religious terms it means saving the soul. In the quest myth it means finding the central point in oneself that is what one is.

Any one of the four artists we have spoken of might give us knowledge enough for our lives. Goethe learned perhaps more than any man who walked this earth has learned, and has fired the imaginations and touched the hearts of both the mighty and the lowly for two centuries. Tributes of personal indebtedness to Wagner have been paid by every one of the great conductors in the central European tradition, by artists labouring in every field, by awed listeners like this one. There have been dedicated Virgilians – often churchmen such as I, teachers and men of letters – in virtually every century since Virgil lived, and they have learned from the poet's compassion for the world's tears and from his searching for answers that had, of their nature and his, always to elude him.

But to me the clearest vision of life has been conveyed by the man said to have been blind. The olive trees in Homer, the swallows and sea eagles, the beautiful women, the imaginative adventures on sea-washed islands, the delicious sense that everything we see means something more than we see without its ever having to be turned to a symbol, the intimations of divine presences, the illuminations, the prayers, the love, the bravery, the generosity, the mystery, the honest tears, the laughter, the wonder, the wonderfully intricate and touching insight into the human nature shared by the hero with his son, his wife, and his father – these seem to this writer more vividly realized, more treasureable, and, in the end, more useful to him in finding himself than what he has found even in his other favoured artists. For thirty-five years this now-retired professor has had the privilege of teaching Homer. And with all his heart he can say, with the lowliest of rhapsodes who recited Homer and only Homer, 'Living your life with Homer, seeing the world through his eyes – that is enough for a life on this fruitful earth.'

Notes

Chapter One

1 The quotations from *The History of Don Quixote de La Mancha* are from the translation by Samuel Putnam found in *Great Books of the Western World*, ed. Mortimer J. Adler, vol. 27 (Chicago: Encyclopaedia Britannica Inc., 1952).

2 I owe the term, and to some extent the insight, to Maria DiBattista, whose chapter 'Don Quixote' appears in Seidel and Mendelson 1977, 103–22.

3 Giamatti 1975, 18

4 Thompson 1966 finds the hero's 'journey to the lower world' in the folklore of Iceland, Ireland, French Canada, Finland, the Jewish diaspora, India, Indonesia, China, the Inuit and native tribes of North America, the native tribes of South America, and in Africa (see his listing F80). He finds a specific 'descent to the world of the dead' in many of the same cultures and in the folklore of Switzerland and Hawaii as well (F81). The journeying hero is accompanied by a companion feature in the folklore of many of the above-mentioned cultures and in the folklore of Italy, Siberia, Mongolia, Turkey, Indonesia, Korea, Japan, and the Philippines as well (F601.1). The hero encounters a 'belle dame sans merci' (G264) in the folklore of seven, and an 'old man helper on the quest' (H1233.1 and N825.2) in the folklore of nine of the above-mentioned cultures. These manifestations, so widely separated in time and space, strongly support the theory of Jung that figures from these cultures, found as well in classic Greek myths and among his patients in twentieth-century

Zurich, are truly archetypal, that is, that they are the product of a collective unconscious, corresponding to something deep in every human psyche, and are not the creations of a single culture that have been disseminated later by tribal migration or commercial intercourse. Critics of Jung continue to insist that neither he nor his disciples have substantiated this claim statistically; Jungian theory still awaits its own Stith Thompson.

5 See Campbell 1956, 18–19, with footnotes.

6 For a positive view of Jungian approaches to mythic works of literature see Frye 1971, especially 108, 193–6, 214, 291, 322–3, and most amusingly the note to 146: 'The atmosphere of critical harrumph about [Jungian typological constructs], which recurs in some forms of archetypal criticism, is not much to the point.'

7 The term is J.H. Finley's (1978, 71).

8 Campbell 1956, 116

9 Campbell 1988, 217

10 The illustration, from manuscript fragment 112 of *Lancelot du Lac* in the Bibliothèque Nationale, is reproduced in Cirlot 1971 as plate XIII.

11 Frye 1990, 214

12 See the elaborate argument in Jackson Knight 1967, 202–25, and the remarkable expansion of the idea in Cruttwell 1971, 83–97. In a recent examination of the labyrinth as symbol, Doob 1990 restates the connection between the *lusus Troiae* in *Aeneid* 5.549–602 and the depiction of a labyrinth marked with the word *truia* on a seventh- or sixth-century BC wine pitcher from Tragliatella (26–8). She also finds several mazes in medieval art and architecture that bear the name 'Troy' (114–16 and 232–3), and demonstrates that the labyrinth functions as a thematic idea throughout the *Aeneid*, both in the wanderings and wars of the hero and in the poet's bleak view of human history (227–53).

Chapter Two

1 J.H. Finley 1978, 6, notes that, before the climactic recognition scene with Odysseus, Penelope 'sleeps six times and dreams three times.' The quotation about the gates of sleep and dreams comes at 19.560–7.

2 N. Austin 1975, 247–51, connects the return of the swallow with the symbolic seasonal concerns of his thesis: the *Odyssey* is both 'our earliest Chelidonismos' and, as comedy 'has its roots in the celebration of spring's victory over winter,' our earliest comedy as well.

3 M.I. Finley 1954, 19, says, most appropriately, that for the Homeric warrior 'there was no weakness, no unheroic trait, but one, and that was cowardice and the consequent failure to pursue heroic goals.'

4 This is the contention of Lord 1963, 36–53.

5 The first half of this observation was formulated by Stanford 1968, 45, in a chapter so perceptive, especially on the encounter of Odysseus with Nausicaa, that the observation is almost disproved.

6 Griffin 1980, 78. Menelaus's 'foolish present,' three horses and a well-polished chariot, is refused by Telemachus as being unsuitable to rocky Ithaca. I've always thought, *pace* Griffin, that it is the nineteen-year-old Telemachus's refusal, and his impatience to be gone, that are, if not quite foolish, more than a little gauche in the light of the elegant hospitality Menelaus has provided. (The fatherless Telemachus is consistently shown as knowing far less about palace manners than does his nineteen-year-old companion Peisistratus, who has had the benefit of Nestor's careful fathering for ten years.) Menelaus might be 'foolish' in offering the horses, but he redeems himself rather wittily when at the boy's refusal he offers instead a piece he had received himself as a token of hospitality – a silver-and-gold mixing bowl. Perhaps with *that* the boy will learn to mix in polite society.

7 So Lloyd-Jones 1991, 30: 'Penguin Books profited hugely from the popular success of the translations by E.V. Rieu (*Odyssey*, 1946; *Iliad*, 1947), who in the words of Adam Parry "discovered that Homer was really Trollope."' Rieu's original 1946 translation is to my mind preferable to the updated but unfortunately toned-down (and not always more correct) revision by his son, published by Penguin in 1991.

8 Martin 1979, 7

9 The *Odyssey* passages that describe the Isles of the Blest (4.566–8) and Mount Olympus (6.42–6) have passed into Arthurian literature by a path we can trace. They were used by Lucretius (3.19–22) to describe the gods' existence in the *intermundia*. Tennyson then used the passage, in the lines I have quoted here, in his *Lucretius* (106–11)

and his *The Passing of Arthur* (428–31). From there the passage was taken up by T.H. White in *The Once and Future King* (1.15) and finally provided the lyrics for the charming title song in Lerner and Loewe's musical *Camelot*.

10 It is possible to think of Odysseus's crew, and especially among them the unventuresome and all-but-mutinous loser Eurylochus, as a kind of shadow-configuration. The wary hero has to rescue his unwary companions from a lotus-induced drug experience and from being turned to beasts by Circe. He almost comes to grief when, despite his strictures, they foolishly open the sack in which Aeolus has enclosed the winds, and he is finally unable to keep them from roasting and eating the proscribed flesh of the oxen of the sun god. While Odysseus is an intellectual quester, his crew are by turns stupid, sensual, greedy, and gluttonous. Yet like a true hero he assumes responsibility for them.

11 Pre-eminently by Beye 1968, 174–8. Feminist commentators have not, so far, exploited this, or made much of the suggestion, advanced by Samuel Butler, that the *Odyssey* may have been written by a woman. Butler, like his friend Bernard Shaw a master at debunking (witness the amusing social satire in *Erewhon*), was struck, when translating the *Odyssey*, by the preponderance of female characters in the narrative and by what he considered the prevailingly feminine perception (that is, that human beings are strongest when they must defend themselves, as women have perennially had to do, from some position of weakness). Butler's witty but seriously intended *The Authoress of the Odyssey* did not convince many readers when it appeared in 1897, but it remains provocative and often insightful. It also became the basis of a novel, *Homer's Daughter*, by Robert Graves, the most amusing section of which is reprinted in Steiner and Fagles 1962, 148–51. David Grene restated the case for Butler's insights in the introduction he wrote for a reprint of the second edition in 1967.

12 This is the etymology suggested by Joseph Russo in Heubeck et al. 1988–92, 3.104, following E. Wüst in Pauly-Wissowa 19.461ff. and H. von Kamptz in *Homerische Personnennamen* (Göttingen, 1982) 29ff. Wüst connected the first part of the name with *pene*, 'thread' or 'woof,' and von Kamptz connected the last part with *olopto*, 'to pluck out.' Penelope's name can thus almost be made to mean 'Weaver-

unraveller,' though von Kamptz finally opted for the more conven-
tional derivation of the name from *penelops*, the wild duck. Manuel
Fernández-Galiano, in Heubeck 3.148, follows von Kamptz, citing
(but without support) the wild duck as 'a model of conjugal fidelity.'

13 J.H. Finley 1978, 8–9, wonders why Homer calls the laugh 'aimless,'
and finds it and the subsequent passing of the hands over the face
'explicable only as prompted by Athene'; both are Penelope's impul-
sive responses to 'the surprise of the inspired moment.' I rather
think, as may become clear in another few paragraphs, that Penelope
really knows as she prepares to appear before the suitors that her husband will be among them in disguise, and that he will see her at last
in her still remarkable beauty. Whitman 1958, 303, would agree with
this partially: for him Penelope does (impulsively?) adorn herself for
her husband, but 'the foolish, empty laugh shows that she does not
really know [that the beggar is he] as yet.'

14 I have published, in a rather different form, this paragraph and some
paragraphs below on the recognition scene between Odysseus and
Penelope in Lee 1979, 135–8.

15 Reece 1993, 185, perceptively says that Telemachus 'realizes that he
has not been able to provide this "disguised god" with proper hospitality ... and so fears divine punishment, hence his plea to spare him.'

16 So Beye 1968, 173, in one of many astute comments.

17 See especially Page 1955, 97–8 and 122–4, and Kirk 1962, 246–7.

18 For a concise discussion of many varying positions, see Russo's commentary on 19.572–81 in Heubeck et al. 1988–92, 3.104. After close
to a half-century I still favour the view of Harsh 1950 (that Penelope
suspects as early as Book 17 that the beggar in her house is Odysseus,
and proceeds immediately but warily to test and, by Book 19, to
cooperate with him). This seems to me preferable to the view of
Amory 1963 (that Penelope first senses the truth subconsciously in
Book 18 when she shows herself to the suitors, and that her awareness thereafter grows through intuitions provided by dreams and
omens) and that of N. Austin 1975 (that Penelope is not entirely sure
of the beggar's identity as late as book 21, when she arranges the con-
test to determine whether what her subconscious tells her is true
really is true). All of these are preferable to the feminist reading of
Murnaghan 1987 (that Penelope is entirely unaware of, even victim-
ized by, events and that the plot is resolved by chance). Other recent

feminist approaches (that Penelope manipulates several simulta-
neous marriage plots) are rejected by Katz 1991, 111–12 and 184–5,
who addresses the ambiguities of Penelope's role via neoanalysis,
'from the perspective of narrative function rather than from that of
psychological verisimilitude.' Her arguments are impressive (certainly they are more than trendy) but beyond the scope of our considerations here. It is of interest to note that the problem with Penelope
was discussed in the first century: Seneca asks, in *Epistles* 88.8, 'Why
ponder whether Penelope was chaste or whether she deceived her
contemporaries, or whether she suspected, before she was certain,
that the man in her presence was Ulysses? Teach me what chastity
is, and what a blessing we have in it, and whether it is found in the
body or the soul.'

19 Dimock 1989, 266, ingeniously suggests that Athene's word *hypo-
dysseai* ('you are about to come out of your evils') may, if 'mis-
divided' as *hyp-odysseai*, be a deliberate pun on Odysseus's name.

20 At the moment (15.482f.) when Odysseus, before going to bed, hears
that his father once sheltered the suppliant Eumaeus, his son, who
has sheltered the suppliant Theoclymenos, eludes the ambush the
suitors have set for him. The poem is not entirely clear on this matter, but it is certainly possible, given the other all-but-telepathic
communications in the poem, to think that something of Odysseus's
father's humanity has been, on the instant of its telling, communicated to Odysseus's son, and that this is the son's salvation. Beye
1968, 168–9, suggests something of this: the boy's rescue of Theo-
clymenus is a sign that he has become a man, and this is 'perhaps
Homer's means of showing what Telemachos has learned from
Nestor at Pylos and Menelaos at Sparta.'

21 Stanford 1968, 57

22 I am indebted for this insight to J.H. Finley 1978, 200.

23 Beye 1975, 94

24 Wisdom 7.22ff.

25 J.H. Finley 1978, 79, notes perceptively that 'the half-cultivated, half-
wild olive sprung from a single root' prefigures the hero's passage
from adventures to 'the new stage' of surviving in a realistic setting.

26 Most trenchant among those who dismiss the last book as un-
Homeric are Page 1955, 102–30, and Kirk 1962, 248–52. But arguments for its being 'an integral part of the compositional plan of the

author who created the *Odyssey* as we know it' are summarized by Heubeck 1988–92, 3.353–5, and expanded in his notes to the important passages *ad loc.* He comments (354) that 'in the last few decades the number of scholars defending the "authenticity" of the conclusion to the *Odyssey* has been steadily rising.' J.H. Finley 1978, 200, suggests that when Aristarchus and Aristophanes called 23.296 the end (*peras* or *telos*) of the poem, they probably meant end 'in the sense of goal.' He rightly adds that 'the particle *men* in the line in any case demands continuation.'

27 Heubeck 1988–92 is of all commentators closest to me here, though he stops short of calling Laertes' mental state madness: 'Odysseus has succeeded in penetrating the wall of apathy with which his father has surrounded himself' (3.393) and 'with well-considered words Odysseus has succeeded in breaking down his father's self-control ... releasing him from the paralysis of emotion, lethargy, and apathy' (3.396). It will be noted that Heubeck does not follow older commentators in interpreting *peiretizōn* (23.221) as 'making trial of' and *kertomiois epeesin* (24.240) as 'with taunting words.' He does not think of Odysseus as cruelly testing his father, and I feel sure that he is right in this.

Chapter Three

1 A useful recent article on the subject is Clark 1991. Some of the same ground was covered earlier, with map and pictures, in Schoder 1971–72. Many further details about the wider area Virgil considers, with accounts from Strabo and others, may be found in McKay 1971, 194–220.

2 See Johnson 1976, esp. 23–48, where, via Lessing, Auerbach, and others, Virgil's almost impressionistic pictures are compared with Homer's more naturalistic style.

3 The plural *animis caelestibus* in Virgil's first question seems to imply a pantheon of gods, a Homeric 'divine machinery,' and on the level of traditional epic narrative it may be so interpreted. (The question *tantaene animis caelestibus irae* is prompted by the first mention of Juno.) On the other hand, the two words may be an example of Virgil's frequent use of 'plural for singular' for emphasis. *Animis caelestibus* may then refer to the Stoic and Virgilian concept of a sin-

gle *deus*, a provident power working in the universe. And that is how I have translated the phrase here. That benevolent power, embodied in Jupiter and usually called *fatum* through most of the epic, turns unpredictably destructive on the penultimate page, when it sends a Dira, a spirit of *furor*, to help the hero kill the enemy who has asked for mercy. Virgil's unanswered question about the supposed goodness of God, *tantaene animis caelestibus irae*, is thus raised again, powerfully and with serious doubts, at the poem's close.

4 Virgil's belief in a largely Stoic but nonetheless individual *deus* has been summarized, as if in a personal credo, on a remarkable page in Wilkinson 1969, 152: 'I believe that there is a power working in the universe. Sometimes I call it simply "natura" ... More often, especially in human and moral contexts, I call it "Jupiter" or "Pater" ... Despite many appearances to the contrary I believe its purposes to be ultimately wise and good; but it cannot work without the co-operation of human effort and prayer ... "Jupiter" is perhaps too anthropomorphic a conception for a divine spirit which, I feel, permeates the whole of nature. The gods of mythology, poetry and popular belief are embodiments of intimations men have had, at various levels, of the working of this power ... Had I tried to dispense with these, I should have felt that an essential element was lacking. I also have numinous feelings about people, notably the Caesars, Julius and Octavian; and if all men have a divine spark, why should not some have a special share?' It seems to me that this accurately represents Virgil's view of divinity during his writing of the mid-career *Georgics*. With the final *Aeneid*, his view is darker, and doubts about the goodness of the Stoic *deus* crowd in on the poet.

5 In Book 6 Virgil has Anchises call the animating power in the universe 'spiritus' (725), 'mens' (726), and, finally, 'deus' (749).

6 Cf. Fredricksmeyer 1984, 14: 'Vergil ... perceives Jupiter as all-powerful, rational, and ultimately benevolent to man. Against this perception militates, however, the experience, ubiquitous in life as in the poem, of evil and suffering, most conspicuously the sufferings of the innocent ... [Vergil] objectifies evil as the main cause of suffering by attributing it to a great cosmic force, Juno ... Since Juno is ultimately subject to the will of Jupiter, the question becomes, finally: how can an all-powerful and benevolent god *allow* the existence in the world of so much evil and undeserved suffering?' In effect, Fredricksmeyer

explains why Virgil used 'plural for singular' in the elusive phrase *tantaene animis caelestibus irae.*

7 C.S. Lewis's *A Preface to Paradise Lost*, with its clear distinctions between 'primary' and 'secondary' epic, was only ten years old at the time, and essential reading for virtually all undergraduate courses in literature.

8 See Servius's praefatio *In Aeneidos Librum 1*, 28 ('Afterwards he wrote the *Aeneid*, proposed by Augustus') and Donatus's *Vita Vergili*, 31 ('Augustus, who it chanced was away campaigning in Spain, demanded in pleading and even playfully intimidating letters that Virgil send him something from the *Aeneid* – either, in his own words, the first *hypographē* or whatever *kōlon* he would like.' Though these statements seem to indicate that Augustus requested the *Aeneid* from Virgil, some modern commentators and critics remain unconvinced. My own view on the matter has been expressed by Stocker 1980, 1–2: 'We must face the fact that it was a commissioned work ... Virgil had an assignment, and this was to write an epic poem in honor of Augustus ... The role, however, should not be too much stressed.'

9 Here we must tread with some caution between Camps 1969, 2 ('It is indeed clear that the figure of Aeneas is intended at times to evoke Octavian; and it is possible that it is substantially modelled on Virgil's conception of Octavian's character ... [I]t will be observed that the picture is not a simple idealization'), and Cairns 1989, 4 (Aeneas and Octavian 'are to be seen as analogous rather than equated').

10 This is the imaginative but not inaccurate translation culled from *verso tenuis cum cardine ventus / impulit et teneras turbavit ianua frondes* (*Aeneid* 3.448–9) by Dickinson 1961, 66.

11 A study of the many father-son relationships in the *Aeneid* is Lee 1979.

12 Cornutus, as quoted in Macrobius *Saturnalia* 5.19.2, used the word *fingere*: *(Vergilius) adsuevit poetico more aliqua fingere ut de aureo ramo.*

13 There is a good discussion of the plant *mōly* (possibly *allium nigrum*, a kind of garlic) and its relation to the Golden Bough in Clark 1979, 209–11. The same volume has well-documented sections on both the bough itself (185–203) and the Cumaean Sibyl (204–11).

14 See Servius on *Aeneid* 6.136 (Thilo and Hagen 1961, 30–1) and Frazer 1951, 1.1–24.

15 Weber 1995, 27, argues that 'the separation of the Golden Bough from its oak is ... a symbolic enactment of the separation of soul from body – that is, of death – without which no journey to Hades is possible.'

16 Segal 1965, 627. In the first part of his remarkably wide-ranging article, published over two years, Segal finds a correspondence between the bough and the inconsolable losses of Icarus, Palinurus, and Misenus. In the second part, he traces the importance of the bough to Aeneas as he journeys through the underworld to the 'philosophical and historical answers' provided by his father Anchises, and thence through the ivory gate. Like the gate, the Golden Bough, 'with its evocation of centuries of human experience condensed into primeval symbolism ... stands ambiguously between civilized man's philosophical solutions to the basic problems of existence and a more direct, unmediated apprehension of the mystery of life and death.' Virgil's symbol, in this reading, provides a 'more basic reality' than do any 'answers' from Greek philosophy and Roman history. See Segal 1966, 69–70.

17 *Anthologia Palatina* 4.1.47–8. The couplet comes in the poem that introduces Meleager's *Stephanos*. A connection between Virgil's Golden Bough and Meleager's description of Platonic philosophy was first suggested by Michels 1945. West 1990, 236–7, uses Meleager's two lines to argue that Virgil's bough is 'the mark of the Eleusinian initiate' and that the bough is golden because it is intended as 'a symbol, for those with ears to hear, of the Platonic contribution to Virgil's great vision.'

18 Donington 1974, 54. See also Jung and Kerényi 1949, 60f., and Jung 1953, passim.

19 See Brooks 1966, 153–4.

20 See Frazer 1951 11.76–94, 279–303, 315–20.

21 See Julius Caesar *De bello Gallico* 6.13–14 and Pliny the Elder *Naturalis Historia* 16.245–51. For Norden's brief comment see Norden 1957, 166.

22 Frazer 1951 mentions the blowing of trumpets in the rituals of Attis (5.268) and Dionysus (7.15), at the Jewish feast of the Purim (9.394), and at the initiation rites of youths in New Guinea (11.249). Clark 1979, 105 n.35, gives further details on the use of trumpets in rituals and seasonal mysteries. The reference to the Jewish sounding of trumpets at the full moon comes in Psalms 81.3.

23 See Servius on *Aeneid* 6.211 (Thilo and Hagen 1961, 40).
24 Williams 1972, 1.472. He finds a similar meaning ('slowly yielding')
   in *Georgics* 2.236 and *Aeneid* 5.856.
25 Fletcher 1941, 45
26 See R.G. Austin 1977, 101.
27 While editions of Virgil may have overlooked the importance of
   volens vis-à-vis *cunctantem*, the journals have not been silent on the
   matter. D'Arms 1964, 267, thinks of the bough as all but animate:
   'The bough "lingers" ... to keep its own beauty intact for a moment
   more.' Segal 1968, 77, goes further: 'The bough suddenly ceases to be
   passive. All at once it manifests a disturbing and mysterious life of
   its own.' More recently, Weber 1995, 6, says: *'ipse volens facilisque
   sequetur* ... is an expression that would ordinarily refer to an animate
   being.' Weber notes that, 'out of sixteen other occurences in Virgil,
   volens ... is applied to gods or to human beings in all cases but one.'
   And, I might add, that one case (*volentia rura* in *Georgics* 2.500) is
   only an apparent exception, as the countryside is all but personified
   in the *Georgics*, and especially in Book 2.
28 The significance of *cunctantem* for the *Aeneid* as a whole has not
   gone unnoticed. See esp. Segal 1990, 4 n.6, and bibliography there.
29 See Norden 1957, *ad loc.*
30 Clausen 1966, 83
31 See *Odyssey* 19.560–7.
32 Fletcher 1941, 101
33 R. G. Austin 1977, 276
34 Servius on *Aeneid* 6.893 (Thilo and Hagen 1961, 122)
35 Quoted in Fletcher 1941, 102. A recent article on the subject, Kilpatrick 1995, provides an extensive bibliography on the gates, and
   argues plausibly and from good evidence that the optical properties of
   horn (transparent) and ivory (opaque) may provide an answer to Virgil's enigma: 'Aeneas' departure via the ivory gate signals that no
   clear images from the dream-vision will ever impinge on his memory' (66). That is in fact what happens: in the six books that follow
   Book 6, Aeneas never consciously adverts to the vision his father
   granted him in the underworld.
36 See Syme 1939, esp. 522–4.
37 Books 1 to 6 of the *Aeneid* have often been thought Virgil's *Odyssey*
   while Books 7 to 12 are, as the very title of Gransden 1984 has it,

Virgil's *Iliad*. (Otis 1964 discusses the poem in two lengthy chapters
entitled 'The Odyssean *Aeneid*' and 'The Iliadic *Aeneid*.') Virgil's
famous opening words, *arma virumque cano* ('Arms and the man I
sing'), could be rendered '*Iliad* and *Odyssey* I sing,' for his Latin *arma*
is close to the *Iliad*'s first word, *mēnin*, and his *virum* is Latin for the
Odyssey's first word, *andra*. Anderson 1969, 8, shows further how
Virgil's *arma* and *virum* interact as a sort of hendiadys, how in the
very first line the ambiguity of the poem is hinted at in two words
that suggest that war can brutalize a man and again that man can use
war for constructive ends.

38 I have cited the parallels in Lee 1979, 14–17, and given further details
on Aeneas's savagery at ibid. 85–8.

39 The most factious controversy in Virgilian studies in recent years has
been that between the so-called Harvard or 'pessimistic' school (perhaps dating from Adam Parry's 'The Two Voices of Virgil's *Aeneid*'
in 1963 and continuing, with varying degrees of commitment, in the
influential writings of Charles Segal, Michael Putnam, William S.
Anderson, W. Ralph Johnson, and others) and what might be called
the Oxbridge, 'optimistic,' or neo-traditionalist school (favoured in
the editions of R.D. Williams and recently given persuasive voice by
Philip Hardie). In the last few years, as the controversy has abated
somewhat, mediating voices have appeared, and on this side of the
Atlantic they have been, most notably, women's voices – Susan Ford
Wiltshire on the *Aeneid* and (armed with 'reader-response criticism')
Christine Perkell on the *Georgics*. These new readings argue that
the ambiguities in Virgil's writing may be, and are intended to be,
left unresolved. For my own part, I have found it easier to read the
Georgics as 'optimistic'; with the *Aeneid* I still find, after a quarter-
century of pondering and teaching the poem, that one reads its ambiguities best as 'sadness at the doubtful doom of humankind.' A brisk
exchange on the matter, between Joseph Farrell and William S.
Anderson, may be found in *Vergilius* 36: 74–81. 'The greatest error,'
Anderson says there, 'is to adopt an either-or position.' The *Aeneid*,
he says, 'is richly dialogic.'

40 Williams 1972, 1.170

41 Lee, 1979, 107

42 Among these are the pioneering Drew 1927, the more cautious

Camps 1969 (esp. 95–104 and 137–43), Tanner 1970–1, Binder 1971, and Alessio 1993.

43 *Inanis* (empty) is here translated 'though [that ceremony] cannot bring him back to life.' The word takes on that meaning as it recurs throughout the poem. See Lee 1979 33–4 and n.7, and the paragraphs Lee is indebted to – Parry 1966, 122–3.

44 The word *inanis* and the shining lilies given the funeral ceremony for Marcellus are part of a remarkable pattern of recurrent words (*miserande puer, pietas, aurum*) and, especially, of images. Compare the shining flowers that cannot bring Marcellus back to life with the Lethean bough passed before Palinurus's eyes in Book 5, with the Golden Bough found during the preparation for Misenus's funeral in Book 6, with the flower cut down by the plough and the poppies burdened with rain that describe the deaths of Euryalus and then of Nisus in Book 9, with the changing colours and drooping neck of the dying Lausus in Book 10, with the virginal violet and hyacinth to which the dead Pallas is compared in Book 11 and, finally, with the dittany stalk in Book 12 that saves Aeneas's life when all around him the cries of young men can be heard in their death agonies. The recurrent words, and especially the flower-images, link the historical Marcellus, the adoptive son of Augustus, with all of the epic's 'sons' of Aeneas who die before their time.

45 The passage has been prepared for by two others, in which the manipulation of motifs is all but Wagnerian: In 12.384–429 Aeneas has been wounded by an arrow, and his doctor, Iapyx the son of Iasus, finds he cannot for all his efforts extract the clinging barb from the flesh, while around the tent the cries of young men dying in battle can be heard. Then Aeneas's mother, clad in mist, appears and plunges a dittany stalk into the water the attendant doctor is using. The arrow then moves of its own accord from the wound. This is, first, a recapitulation of motifs from the passage on the helmsman Palinurus (where Venus intervenes for her son, the god of sleep comes clad in mist, a Lethean bough plunges Palinurus – another son of Iasus – into the water even though he clings to the rudder, and as he cries out to his companions the ship moves of its own accord on its course). It is also a forecast of the events at 12.746–87, where Aeneas, slowed by the arrow-wound, sees his spear lodged in a tree

sacred to those saved from shipwreck, and cannot remove it for all his efforts till his mother Venus intervenes to pluck it out for him. For a discussion of these and other subtleties in the final pages of the epic see Lee 1981/2, 13–16.

46 Lee 1979, 192, quotes two of those who have felt it necessary to round off the story: 'The road is now open for what Pliny called "the boundless majesty of the Roman peace"' (R.D. Williams) and 'All bitterness and all passion was now laid at rest, and all could now join hands as comrades and together walk to meet the shining future' (Moses Hadas). These *lieti finali* were anticipated in the fifteenth century by the twenty-year-old Maphaeus Vegius, who wrote a thirteenth book so Virgilian in its style (and so appealing to Renaissance sensibility) that it appeared in editions of Virgil for more than a century. Vegius settles affairs between the Trojans and their enemies and sees Aeneas to his death and apotheosis. That, I submit, was never Virgil's intent.

47 Some commentators, citing Donatus 35, have thought that Virgil, had he lived past the year 19 B.C., would have extended the *Aeneid* beyond the twelfth book. But Donatus 35 records only that that year Virgil still wished to give the poem its finishing touches (*summa manus*). And we are told in Donatus 23 that when Virgil planned his epic he wrote a complete outline in prose and divided it into twelve books, no more, before he began versifying. Further, the patterns of imagery indicated in notes 44 and 45 above and the succession of episodes that close Book 12 – the decision of Turnus to rise heroically to meet his fate, the resolution of the conflict between Jupiter and Juno, the surprising reversal when Jupiter sends the Dira to earth, the even more surprising reversal when Aeneas kills Turnus (*fatum* and *pietas* give way to *furor* in these episodes) – all of this seems designed to make a compelling, powerful, and ambivalent conclusion. There is no evidence that Virgil intended the *Aeneid* to end otherwise than it does.

48 Augustus was the adoptive son of Julius Caesar. After Caesar's assassination, Augustus, who had killed off his enemies, implemented the plans for a Roman peace that his adoptive father had initiated. He may be thought to have heeded what Virgil was saying at the end of the *Aeneid*, and to have learned from his poet.

49 Eliot 1961 (1944), 73

50 Eliot 1961 (1951), 137. The German writer Eliot is indebted to here is
   Theodor Haecker.
51 Giammati 1975, 19 and 23

Chapter Four

1 Part of this chapter has appeared, in an altered and considerably
   shorter form, in Lee 1995, 123–36.
2 Steiner 1989, 167
3 Loomis 1963, 2, sums up the various claims with characteristically
   understated wit: 'The quest of the Grail has led to the Punjab in
   India, to the palace of Atreus at Mycenae and the temple of Zeus at
   Dodona, to the monastery of Montserrat in Spain, to the palace of
   Chosroes in Persia, and the Christian shrines of Constantinople. Pick
   up a book on the subject, and you may be told, with a great show of
   erudition, that the object itself was derived from the cauldron of the
   Irish god Dagda, from the eye of the Egyptian god Thoth, from a symbol of the female organ of generation, from a pearl of the Zoroastrian
   cult named Gohar, from a talisman of the heretical Albigensians,
   once adored in a cavern of the Pyrenees, or from a "Great Sapphire,"
   formerly preserved in the sacristy of Glastonbury Abbey. On the
   other hand, there are those scholars who are content to believe that
   the Grail was *ab origine* conceived as a peculiarly holy eucharistic
   vessel.'
4 In a letter written to Mathilde Wesendonck on 30 May 1859, Wagner
   complains at length that Wolfram 'has understood absolutely nothing of the actual content' of the mythic events he narrates. See Spencer and Millington 1987, 456–60.
5 There is no evidence that Wagner read Robert de Boron. Apart from
   Wolfram, his main source for the Grail legends was a summary of
   Albrecht von Scharfenberg's *The Younger Titurel*, included in San-
   Marte's translation of Wolfram's *Willehalm*. The Grail there is
   identified with Joseph of Arimathea's cup.
6 Loomis 1963, 5–6, remarks that, though the early Arthurian
   romances are set in England and Wales, they were all, with the sole
   exception of the *Peredur*, composed on the continent. On the basis of
   evidence both external and internal he concludes (13–14) that 'the
   conteurs of the twelfth and early thirteenth century were in the main

Bretons, descendants of those Britons who in the fifth and six century, as a result of the Anglo-Saxon invasion, had emigrated to Armorica, which we now know as Brittany.'

7 Waite 1933, 27, cites Grail legends from France, Germany, England and Wales, Holland, Italy, Spain, and Portugal. The geographical spread within the stories is even more remarkable. In the first pages of Wolfram, Parzifal's father Gamuret travels eastwards to Bagdad (Baldac) and Egyptian Alexandria and westwards to Spain. In the last pages, Parzifal's mulatto Asian half-brother Feirefiz, appropriately baptized, travels to India and begets Prester John.

8 A voluminous defence of this point of view, impressively researched, is Waite 1933. In the face of the many hypotheses that would derive the Grail legends from various pagan antecedents, he says (314), 'I am convinced ... that the faculty of invention was militantly alive in the twelfth and thirteenth centuries and that it is folly to account for its creations by the prodigal multiplication of suppostitious lost texts which were held to contain the inventions in some variant or identical form.'

9 See Weston 1957, 75–6.

10 Chrétien's variant of this – his king has been wounded in the buttocks – seems an attempt merely to avoid an indelicacy in his source that the less fastidious Wolfram is quite ready to accept.

11 This comes in Book III (section 140 in Mustard and Passage 1961). Wolfram's etymology is questionable, but no more so than Wagner's when in Act II of *Parsifal* he derives the hero's name from the Persian *fal parsi* or 'pure fool.' The medieval devotion to the pierced heart of Jesus is illustrated (from relatively late woodcuts and paintings) on the plates facing pages 65, 96, 97, 160, and 161 in Jung and von Franz 1970.

12 See Newman 1949, 670–5.

13 See Jackson Knight 1967, 253–8 and n.32. A good deal of Cruttwell's approbation of Wagner was quoted directly by Jackson Knight in his original *Cumaean Gates* 1936, 143–4. After Jackson Knight's death the words of Cruttwell were paraphrased (and perhaps intentionally de-emphasized) by the editor of the 1967 volume.

14 Loomis 1927, 294

15 Beckett 1981, 18

16 Wagner's Kundry also contains, from outside the tradition of the

Grail stories, features of Herodias (turned in German legends to a Wild Rider), Mary Magdalen (driven by repentence to wash Jesus' feet with her tears and dry them with her hair), the Wandering Jew (punished with eternal wandering for having laughed at Christ carrying his cross), and Savitri (released by Buddha from endless cycles of reincarnation).

17 Wagner accepted the dubious etymology of Joseph von Görres, who edited the legends of Lohengrin. See Müller and Wapnewski 1992, 84.

18 The quotations from Nietzsche that follow are taken from various translators in Beckett 1981, 113–15.

19 We need not suppose that it was Wagner's rearrangement of Christianity for his own purposes in *Parsifal* that offended Nietzsche. It was Christianity itself. A year after the final, violent outburst against Wagner's opera, Nietzsche wrote, in *The Anti-Christ* (1888): 'I *condemn* Christianity, I bring against the Christian Church the most terrible charge any prosecutor has ever uttered. To me it is the extremest thinkable form of corruption ... The Christian Church has left nothing untouched by its depravity, it has made of every value a disvalue, of every truth a lie, of every kind of integrity a vileness of soul.' (Beckett 1981, 114–15)

20 As a professional Christian, my initial problems with the work lay in what seemed to me its dubious parallels between Jesus and Parsifal/Amfortas and its presumptuous use of Christian symbols to exalt a private religion of art, with Wagner as the glorified artist. Later I had to wrestle with what Wapnewski (Müller and Wapnewski 1992, 91) has called the opera's 'hostility to the senses and to women.' (*Parsifal* for Wapnewski 'is a profoundly inhuman spectacle, glorifying a barren masculine world whose ideals are a combination of militarism and monasticism.') It took a reading of Chrétien and Wolfram and a performance of the legendary Wieland Wagner production under Hans Knappertsbusch at Bayreuth in 1963 to win me finally to the work. The multilevelled *Parsifal* simply cannot be comprehended with attention fixed exclusively on a single aspect. The opera is like the Grail it celebrates: some draw sustenance from it, some are blinded by it, some fail to understand it, and some can never see it even when in its presence.

21 For the quotations from Mahler and Wolf see Millington 1992, 381; that from Sibelius see Hodson 1984, 133.

22 An extensive Jungian analysis of the Parsifal legends, especially in Chrétien and Wolfram, is E. Jung and von Franz 1970. An earlier and unnecessarily complicated Jungian analysis of Wagner's opera, written by Hans Grunsky for the Bayreuth program when the festival reopened in 1951, is summarized in Müller and Wapnewski 1992, 142.

23 Frye 1971, 193–4. There are also in *Parsifal* some very striking anticipations of Freud: the association of the mother-image with sexual awakening (also present in *Siegfried*) and the affinity between sexuality and religious ecstasy (shocking in 1882, widely accepted now).

24 Chastity has greater importance for Wagner's Grail knights than for Wolfram's. In the medieval poet, the writing that appears on the Grail stone summons both male and female votaries, and though all of them live chaste ascetic lives, the women marry after their initiation, while the men are allowed wives on their missions to lands in need, and the Grail king is allowed to marry the woman indicated for him by the Grail writing. Wagner's greater emphasis on chastity is the result of his need to simplify his material (always the case), his own personal difficulties with sexuality (often the case), and the importance to him of Schopenhauer's concept of *Wille* (the case with all of his works after *Tristan und Isolde*). A brief but insightful discussion of this matter may be found in Müller and Wapnewski 1992, 265–6.

25 See Frye 1990, 352: 'Schopenhauer was probably another Oedipal father whom Nietzsche wanted to kill.'

26 That Wagner's idea of compassion is central in the sources as well is emphasized by Campbell 1988, 116: 'The big moment in the medieval myth is the awakening of the heart to compassion, the transformation of passion into compassion. That is the whole problem of the Grail stories, compassion for the wounded king. And out of that you get the notion that Abelard offered as an explanation of the crucifixion: that the Son of God came down into this world to be crucified to awaken our hearts to compassion, and thus to turn our minds from the gross concerns of raw life in the world to the specifically human values of self-giving in shared suffering. In that sense the wounded king, the maimed king of the Grail legend, is a counterpart of the Christ. He is there to evoke compassion and thus bring a dead wasteland to life.' Campbell was no Wagnerite, but here he is close to Wagner's ideas in *Parsifal*.

27 Küng 1982, 123, where the paraphrased statement from Toynbee is cited.

28 The pervasive influence of the Classics on Wagner was a subject neglected for the better part of a century. The best recent treatments are Lloyd-Jones 1982 and Roller 1992.

29 For recent, often differing assessments of Wagner's social, philosophical, and political opinions see Deathridge and Dahlhaus 1984, 68–87, the short essays in Millington 1992, 140–9 and 153–64, and the longer pieces in Müller and Wapnewski 1992, 166–201. For an extended, dated (that is to say, for the main part, biassed) but compulsively readable account of the interaction of music and theoretical ideas during the writing of *Parsifal*, see the chapters '*Parsifal* and Polemics' and 'Moral Collapse' in Gutman 1968, 389–440. Gutman is refuted at some length by Beckett 1981, 121–3, and with appropriate briefness (he is even kept anonymous) by Hartmut Reinhardt in Müller and Wapnewski 1992, 294–5.

30 The best short book on Wagner's influence and on other aspects of his art is still Magee 1988. A good collection of essays on the influence of Wagner's ideas on intellectual and cultural movements in both Europe and America is Large and Weber 1984.

31 I find the attempts of Gutman and others to denigrate *Parsifal* because Wagner composed it, a drama of renunciation, amid satin and attar of roses supplied by his penultimate mistress, Judith Gautier, either beneath contempt or beside the point. As with several other artists of importance, a symbiosis existed between Wagner's composing and the characters he composed for. A storm at sea prompted his *Fliegende Holländer*; his *Tannhäuser* presaged much of his career for the decade to follow; the historical element in *Lohengrin* bespeaks his hope for a united Germany and his political involvement in the revolution in Dresden in 1848. He fell in love to create the love music of Act II of *Tristan* and moved to decaying Venice to write the death agonies of Act III. As for *Parsifal*, Amfortas in the sources is quilted in silk, and the fevered air around him sweetened by scent as he suffers. Wagner recreated that atmosphere to write some of *Parsifal*. But more to the point, he suffered from chronic skin disorders, deteriorating health, and recurrent heart attacks as he wrote it. He was racing against time to finish it. That seems to me to be more relevant to understanding the work than the

fact that he needed quiet and physical stimulation to keep at the writing of it.

32 From *Art and Revolution* (1848). The translation is my own.

33 This is the opening statement in *Religion und Kunst* (1880). The translation is my own.

34 From the letter of 31 January 1883. The translation is my own.

35 See Beckett 1981, 146–7. Similarly, Roger Loomis (1963, 276) summarizes Wolfram's poem in terms that sound like a description of Wagner's opera: 'Progress from ignorance, self-absorption and anger to understanding, humility and compassion.'

Chapter Five

1 Quoted in Wayne 1959, 18; trans. Alexander Dru

2 Dieckmann 1972, 64, expresses the opinion that 'There can be no doubt that Wagner did not give life to the creature he believes to be his work. Life in the test tube starts only when Mephistopheles enters the laboratory ... It takes the devil to create man.'

3 The *Urfaust* contains Faust's evocation of the Earth-Spirit and subsequent encounter with Wagner; the appearance of Mephistopheles as a professor; the interlude in Auerbach's Cellar, and virtually all of the Gretchen sequence (although, without the voice from heaven crying 'Gerettet!' at the end, the Gretchen of the *Urfaust* is apparently damned). There is no prologue in the theatre, no prelude in heaven, no Walpurgisnacht, nothing of Part Two. But the most remarkable thing about the *Urfaust* is not how little it has of the complete *Faust* but how little it owes to the earlier Faust tradition.

4 Rexroth 1969, 21

5 Heller 1952, 35

6 Quoted by Heller 1965, 25

7 Mann 1968, 186

8 Quoted in Wayne 1949, 19

9 Because I hope to convey something of the feel of Goethe's verses I have left some of the translations in verse; these are from Wayne 1949 and 1959. The prose translations within the text are my own.

10 See Pelikan 1995, 7.

11 A good discussion of various interpretations of the Earth-Spirit is Mason 1967, esp. 110–78.

12 Karl Viëtor, quoted in Spender 1958, xvii

13 Though Goethe told Eckermann (in the conversation on 10 January 1830) that the concept of the Mothers came from Plutarch, he has clearly made from the concept a myth of his own. The Plutarch works in question are possibly *Marcellus* and *On the Cessation of the Oracles*. See Jantz 1969, esp. 31 and 87. Pelikan 1995, 48–50, noting that Goethe's myth of the Mothers has been seen both as a parody, 'a joking pseudo-myth,' and as 'the most transcendental scene that Goethe ever attempted,' interpets it in terms of Goethe's pantheistic idea of Nature and as contributing symbolically to the drama's final revelation of the Eternal Feminine.

14 See Fairley 1953, 110 ff., who succinctly states the many questions we will be faced with in the fifth and last act of *Faust*: 'Is the Philemon and Baucis episode intended to rebut the argument or to illustrate it? Is the blinding of Faust a defeat or a victory? Does he see clearly in his dying moments or is he deluded? Did he win the wager or did he lose it? Is the saving of Faust a judgement or a reward? Does the poem go orthodox at the last or does it not?'

15 Heller 1965, 36

16 Wilkinson and Willoughby 1962, 106

17 Pelikan 1995, 110

18 Rather 1959, 62, finds traces of this dubious reading in a commentary as recent as 1949, and adds, 'It is said that Hitler took particular pleasure in this part of *Faust*. Obviously, he saw in it a precedent, if not a justification, for his own ruthlessness. If a few innocent bystanders were hurt by the tempestuous strivings of the Faustian man, so much the worse for them.'

19 Conversation with Eckermann of 6 June 1831; quoted in Pelikan 1995, 95

20 In the conversation of 6 June 1831, recorded in Fairley 1953, 117

21 See Pelikan 1995, 116, who, discussing the importance of the Catholic symbolism, quotes from Günther Müller ('It would be forcing things to exclude echoes of this completely') and H.S. Jantz (We see here 'that loving fusion of pagan and Christian convictions in which Goethe ... found his own final religious peace').

22 Quoted in Mason 1967, 373. The statement was made on 6 June 1831.

23 Quoted in ibid. For Goethe's views on the importance, indeed the necessity, of religious belief see Bergstraesser 1969, esp. 150.

24 Quoted in Mason 1967, 375–6. The statement was made on 6 May 1827.
25 A perceptive essay along these lines is L.A. Willoughby, 'Goethe's *Faust*: A Morphological Approach,' in Wilkinson and Willoughby 1962, 95–117.
26 Heller 1952, 42
27 Quoted in Rather 1959, 64
28 Quoted in Heller 1952, 31

Chapter Six

1 Don Quixote's niece was quite right to be suspicious, not only of the romances of chivalry on her uncle's shelves, but of the pastoral books as well. In the penultimate chapter of Cervantes's long novel, the old man, cured of his questing illusion, hopes to realize in its stead the pastoral dream. Don Alonso Quijano the Good, once known as Don Quixote de la Mancha the knight-errant, will become Don Quixotiz the shepherd. He is encouraged to indulge this fantasy by, once again, the priest and the barber, and by the very man of letters, Sansón Carrasco, who had defeated him, for his own good, in his last adventure as knight-errant. There is some reason in their redirecting Don Quixote's ideal: the pastoral dream can be acted out in nearby fields, while questing ends Lord knows where. And whether they realize it or not, the pastoral like the quest is a means of self-discovery: a pastoral poet projects himself on a landscape of his own imagination, and so prepares himself (as Virgil, Spenser, Milton, and Goethe did) for larger literary quests.
2 The last and best requiem for them, I think, was the 1937 film of Jean Renoir, *La Grande Illusion*, made as a plea for understanding and peace on the eve of the Second World War in terms of the end of chivalry's ideals and symbols in the First World War.
3 See lecture 8 to the London Philosophical Society (in *Lectures on the Principles of Judgement, Culture, and European Literature*, 1818) and *Table Talk* (11 August 1832).
4 Vinaver 1980, 140
5 Norman 1969, 203, using Dona Luisa and Ananda K. Coomara-swamy.
6 Vann 1962, 7

7 Kerényi is quoted in Vann (above). In Eliade 1968, 141–4, not only does the world 'speak to man' but 'man answers it by his dreams and his imaginative life.'

8 Quoted in Vann 1959, 13–14

9 Vann 1962, 13–14

10 From 'Ithaca,' by C.P. Cavafy; trans. Rae Dalven

Select Bibliography

Alessio, Maria. 1993. *Studies in Vergil: Aeneid Eleven, an Allegorical Approach*. Laval, Que.: Montfort & Villeroy

Amory, Anne. 1963. 'The Reunion of Odysseus and Penelope.' In Taylor 1963, 100–21

Anderson, William S. 1969. *The Art of the Aeneid*. Englewood Cliffs, NJ: Prentice-Hall

– 1990. 'Response.' *Vergilius* 36: 80–1

Ashe, Geoffrey, ed. 1971 (1968). *The Quest for Arthur's Britain*. St Albans: Paladin

Atkins, Stuart. 1958. *Goethe's Faust: A Literary Analysis*. Cambridge: Harvard University Press

Auerbach, Erich. 1953 (1912). *Mimesis: The Representation of Reality in Western Literature*. Trans. Willard Trask. Princeton: Princeton University Press

Austin, Norman. 1975. *Archery at the Dark of the Moon: Poetic Problems in Homer's Odyssey*. Berkeley: University of California Press

Austin, R.G., ed. 1977. *Aeneidos Liber Sextus*. Oxford: Clarendon Press

Bailey, George. 1972. *Germans: Biography of an Obsession*. New York: World Publishing

Beckett, Lucy. 1981. *Richard Wagner: Parsifal*. Cambridge: Cambridge University Press

Bergemann, F., ed. 1955. *Johann Peter Eckermann: Gespräche mit Goethe*. Wiesbaden: Insel-Verlag

Bergstraesser, Arnold C. 1969. 'The Nature of Man.' In Vickery and Sellery 1969, 143–50

Beye, Charles Rowan. 1968 (1966). *The Iliad, the Odyssey, and the Epic Tradition*. London: Macmillan
– 1975. *Ancient Greek Literature and Society*. Garden City, NY: Anchor Press / Doubleday
Binder, Gerhard. 1971. *Aeneas und Augustus: Interpretationen zum 8. Buch der Aeneis*. Meisenheim am Glan: A. Hain
Blissett, William. 1979. 'The Liturgy of *Parsifal*.' *University of Toronto Quarterly* 49: 117–38
Bodkin, Maud. 1958 (1934). *Archetypal Patterns in Poetry*. New York: Vintage Books
Broch, Hermann. 1977 (1946). *The Death of Virgil*. Trans. Jean Starr Untermeyer. London: Routledge and Kegan Paul
Brooks, Robert A. 1966 (1953). '*Discolor Aura*: Reflections on the Golden Bough.' In Commager 1966, 143–63
Burbidge, Peter, and Richard Sutton, ed. 1979. *The Wagner Companion*. New York: Cambridge University Press
Butler, Samuel. 1967 (1897). *The Authoress of the Odyssey*. Chicago: University of Chicago Press
Cairns, Francis. 1989. *Virgil's Augustan Epic*. Cambridge: Cambridge University Press
Campbell, Joseph. 1956 (1949). *The Hero with a Thousand Faces*. New York: World Publishing Company
Campbell, Joseph, and Bill Moyers. 1988. *The Power of Myth*. New York: Doubleday
Camps, W.A. 1969. *An Introduction to Virgil's Aeneid*. London: Oxford University Press
Cavafy, C.P. 1961. *The Complete Poems of Cavafy*. Trans. Rae Dalven. New York: Harcourt, Brace & World
Chetwynd, Tom. 1982. *A Dictionary of Symbols*. London: Granada Publishing Company
Cirlot, J.E. 1971 (1962). *A Dictionary of Symbols*. Trans. Jack Sage. New York: Philosophical Library
Clark, Raymond J. 1979. *Catabasis: Vergil and the Wisdom-Tradition*. Amsterdam: B.G. Grüner
– 1991. 'Virgil's Poetic Treatment of Cumaean Geography.' *Vergilius* 37: 60–8
Clausen, Wendell. 1966 (1964). 'An Interpretation of the *Aeneid*.' In Commager 1966, 75–88

Commager, Steele, ed. 1966. *Virgil: A Collection of Critical Essays*. Englewood Cliffs, NJ: Prentice-Hall

Conington, John (rev. Henry Nettleship). 1963 (1863). *The Works of Virgil*. 4th ed., vol 2. Hildesheim: Georg Olms Verlagsbuchhandlung

Cruttwell, Robert W. 1971 (1947). *Virgil's Mind at Work: An Analysis of the Symbolism of the Aeneid*. Westport, Conn.: Greenwood Press

Dahlhaus, Carl. 1979. *Richard Wagner's Music Dramas*. Trans. Mary Whittall. Cambridge: Cambridge University Press

Dalzell, A. 1956. 'Maecenas and the Poets.' *Phoenix* 10: 151–62

D'Arms, John H. 1964. 'Vergil's "Cunctantem (Ramum)"': *Aeneid* 6.211.' *Classical Journal* 59: 265–7

Deathridge, John, and Carl Dahlhaus. 1984. *The New Grove Wagner*. New York: W.W. Norton

DiBattista, Maria. 1977. 'Don Quixote.' In Seidel and Mendelson 1977, 105–22

Dickinson, Patric, trans. 1961. *Vergil: The Aeneid*. New York: Mentor

Dieckmann, Liselotte. 1972. *Goethe's Faust: A Critical Reading*. Englewood Cliffs, NJ: Prentice-Hall

Dimock, George E. 1989. *The Unity of the Odyssey*. Amherst: University of Massachusetts Press

Donington, Robert. 1974 (1963). *Wagner's 'Ring' and Its Symbols*. London: Faber and Faber

Doob, Penelope Reed. 1990. *The Idea of the Labyrinth*. Ithaca: Cornell University Press

Drew, D.L. 1927. *The Allegory of the Aeneid*. Oxford: Blackwell

Eliade, Mircea. 1968 (1963). *Myth and Reality*. Trans. Willard R. Trask. New York: Harper and Row

Eliot, T.S. 1961 (1944). 'What Is a Classic?' In *On Poetry and Poets*. New York: Farrar, Straus & Cudahy

– 1961 (1951). 'Virgil and the Christian World.' In *On Poetry and Poets*

– 1961 (1955). 'Goethe as the Sage.' In *On Poetry and Poets*

Fairley, Barker. 1953. *Goethe's Faust: Six Essays*. Oxford: Clarendon Press

Farrell, Joseph. 1990. 'Which *Aeneid* in Whose Nineties?' *Vergilius* 36: 74–80

Fergusson, Francis. 1966 (1956). '"Myth" and the Literary Scruple.' In Vickery 1966, 139–47

Finley, John H., Jr. 1978. *Homer's Odyssey*. Cambridge: Harvard University Press

Finley, M.I. 1954. *The World of Odysseus.* New York: Viking Press

Fletcher, Sir Frank. 1941. *Virgil: Aeneid VI.* Oxford: Oxford University Press

Frazer, Sir James George. 1951 (1911, orig. 1890). *The Golden Bough.* 3rd ed., 11 vols. London: Macmillan

Fredricksmeyer, E.A. 1984. 'On the Opening of the *Aeneid.*' *Vergilius* 30: 10–18

Frye, Northrop. 1966 (1951). 'The Archetypes of Literature.' In Vickery 1966, 139–47

– 1971 (1957). *Anatomy of Criticism.* Princeton: Princeton University Press

– 1990. *Myth and Metaphor.* Charlotteville and London: University Press of Virginia

Giamatti, A. Bartlett. 1966. *The Earthly Paradise and the Renaissance Epic.* Princeton: Princeton University Press

– 1975. *A Play of Double Senses: Spenser's Faerie Queene.* Englewood Cliffs, NJ: Prentice-Hall

– 1984. *Exile and Change in Renaissance Literature.* New Haven: Yale University Press

Gillies, Alexander. 1957. *Goethe's Faust: An Interpretation.* Oxford: Basil Blackwell

Gransden, K.W. 1984. *Virgil's Iliad: An Essay on Epic Narrative.* Cambridge: Cambridge University Press

Gregor-Dellin, Martin. 1980. *Richard Wagner: His Life, His Work, His Century.* Trans. J. Maxwell Brownjohn. New York: Harcourt, Brace, Jovanovich

Griffin, Jasper. 1980. *Homer on Life and Death.* Oxford: Clarendon Press

Gutman, Robert W. 1968. *Richard Wagner: The Man, His Mind, and His Music.* New York: Harcourt, Brace

Haecker, Theodor. 1931. *Vergil, Vater des Abendlandes.* Leipzig: Jacob Hegner

Hardie, Philip R. 1986. *Virgil's Aeneid: Cosmos and Imperium.* Oxford: Clarendon Press

Harrison, S.J. 1990. *Oxford Readings in Vergil's Aeneid.* Oxford: Oxford University Press

Harsh, Philip Whaley. 1950. 'Penelope and Odysseus in *Odyssey* XIX.' *American Journal of Philology* 71: 1–21

Heller, Erich. 1952. *The Disinherited Mind.* Cambridge: Bowes and Bowes

– 1965. *The Artist's Journey into the Interior*. New York: Random House

Heubeck, Alfred, Stephanie West, J.B. Hainsworth, Arie Hoekstra, Joseph Russo, and Manuel Fernández-Galiano, ed. 1988–92. *A Commentary on Homer's Odyssey*. 3 vols. Oxford: Clarendon Press

Hodson, Phillip. 1984. *Who's Who in Wagner*. New York: Macmillan

Jackson Knight, W.F. 1944. *Roman Vergil*. London: Faber and Faber

– 1967 (1932–9). *Vergil: Epic and Anthropology*. Ed. John D. Christie. London: Allen & Unwin

Jantz, Harold. 1969. *The Mothers in Faust: The Myth of Time and Creativity*. Baltimore: Johns Hopkins Press

Johnson, W.R. 1976. *Darkness Visible: A Study of Vergil's Aeneid*. Berkeley: University of California Press

Jung, C.G. 1953. *Psychology and Alchemy*. Trans. R.F.C. Hull. London: Pantheon Books

Jung, C.G., and C. Kerényi. 1949. *Essays on a Science of Mythology*. New York: Harper and Row

Jung, Emma, and Marie-Louise von Franz. 1970. *The Grail Legend*. Trans. Andrea Dykes. New York: G.P. Putnam's Sons

Katz, Marylin A. 1991. *Penelope's Renown: Meaning and Indeterminacy in the Odyssey*. Princeton: Princeton University Press

Kilpatrick, Ross S. 1995. 'The Stuff of Doors and Dreams.' *Vergilius* 41: 63–70

Kirk, G.S. 1962. *The Songs of Homer*. Cambridge: University Press

Klindworth, Karl, arr. 1904. *Richard Wagner: Parsifal*. Piano score. New York: G. Schirmer

Küng, Hans. 1982. 'The Yearning for Redemption.' In *Parsifal: Programmheft I*, 114–28. Bayreuth: Verlag der Festspielleitung

Lange, Victor. 1968. *Goethe: A Collection of Critical Essays*. Englewood Cliffs, NJ: Prentice-Hall

Large, David C., and William Weber, ed. 1984. *Wagnerism in European Culture and Politics*. Ithaca: Cornell University Press

Lee, M. Owen. 1979. *Fathers and Sons in Virgil's Aeneid*. Albany: State University of New York Press

– 1981. 'The Sons of Iasus and the End of the *Aeneid*.' *The Augustan Age* 1: 13–16

– 1995. *First Intermissions*. New York: Oxford University Press

Levin, Jerome D. 1992. *Theories of the Self*. Washington: Taylor and Francis

Lloyd-Jones, Hugh. 1976. 'Wagner and the Greeks.' *Times Literary Supplement*, 9 January: 3–39 (revised 1982 in *Blood for the Ghosts*, 126–42. London: Duckworth)

– 1991. 'Welcome Homer!' *New York Review of Books*, 14 February: 28–33

Loomis, Roger Sherman. 1927. *Celtic Myth and Arthurian Romance*. New York: Columbia University Press

– 1963. *The Grail: From Celtic Myth to Christian Symbol*. Cardiff: University of Wales Press

Lord, George de F. 1963 (1954). 'The *Odyssey* and the Western World.' In Taylor 1963, 36–53

McCune, Marjorie W., Orbison Tucker, and Philip M. Within, ed. 1980. *The Binding of Proteus: Perspectives on Myth and the Literary Process*. Lewisburg: Bucknell University Press

McKay, A.G. 1971 (1970). *Vergil's Italy*. Bath: Adams and Dart

– 1972. *Ancient Campania I: Cumae and the Phlegraean Fields*. Hamilton, Ont.: Vergilian Society

Magee, Bryan. 1988 (1968). *Aspects of Wagner*. Oxford: Oxford University Press

Mann, Thomas. 1968 (1939) *Lotte in Weimar*. Trans. H.T. Lowe-Porter. Harmondsworth: Penguin Books

– 1985 (1902–51). *Pro and Contra Wagner*. Trans. Allan Blunden. London: Faber and Faber

Martin, George. 1979. *The Opera Companion to Twentieth-Century Opera*. New York: Dodd, Mead & Company

Mason, Eudo C. 1967. *Goethe's Faust: Its Genesis and Purport*. Berkeley: University of California Press

Michels, Agnes K. 1945. 'The Golden Bough of Plato.' *American Journal of Philology* 66: 59–63

Millington, Barry. 1987. *Wagner*. New York: Vintage Books

Millington, Barry, ed. 1992. *The Wagner Compendium*. New York: Schirmer Books

Moorman, Charles. 1969. 'Myth and Medieval Literature: *Sir Gawain and the Green Knight*.' In Vickery 1966, 171–86

– 1980. 'Comparative Mythology: A Fungo in the Outfield.' In McCune 1980, 63–77

Müller, Ulrich, and Peter Wapnewski, ed. 1992. *Wagner Handbook*. Cambridge: Harvard University Press

Murnaghan, Sheila. 1987. *Disguise and Recognition in the Odyssey*. Princeton: Princeton University Press

Mustard, Helen M., and Charles E. Passage. Trans. 1961. *Wolfram von Eschenbach: Parzifal*. New York: Vintage Books

Nelson, Conny. 1969. *Homer's Odyssey: A Critical Handbook*. Belmont, Calif.: Wadsworth Publishing

Newman, Ernest. 1949. *Wagner Nights*. London: Putnam & Company

− 1976 (1937). *The Life of Richard Wagner*. 4 vols. Cambridge: Cambridge University Press

Norden, Eduard. 1957 (1916). *Aeneis: Buch VI*. 4th ed. Darmstadt: Wissenschaftliche Buchgesellschaft

Norman, Dorothy. 1969. *The Hero: Myth/Image/Symbol*. New York: Doubleday

Otis, Brooks. 1964. Virgil: *A Study in Civilized Poetry*. Oxford: Clarendon Press

Page, Denys. 1955. *The Homeric Odyssey*. Oxford: Clarendon Press

Parry, Adam. 1966 (1963). 'The Two Voices of Virgil's *Aeneid*.' In Commager 1966, 107–23

Pelikan, Jaroslav. 1995. *Faust the Theologian*. New Haven: Yale University Press

Perkell, Christine. 1989. *The Poet's Truth: A Study of the Poet in Virgil's Georgics*. Berkeley: University of California Press

Raglan, Lord. 1956 (1936). *The Hero: A Study in Tradition, Myth, and Drama*. New York: Random House

Rather, L.J. 1959. 'Some Reflections on the Philemon and Baucis Episode in Goethe's *Faust*.' *Diogenes* 25: 60–73

Reece, Steve. 1993. *The Stranger's Welcome: Oral Theory and the Aesthetics of the Homeric Hospitality Scene*. Ann Arbor: University of Michigan Press

Rexroth, Kenneth. 1969. 'Goethe.' *Saturday Review*, April 19: 21

Rieu, E.V., trans. 1946. *Homer: The Odyssey*. Harmondsworth: Penguin

Roller, Duane W. 1992. 'Richard Wagner and the Classics.' *Euphrosyne* NS 20: 231–52

Sandars, N.K. 1972. *The Epic of Gilgamesh*. Harmondsworth: Penguin Books

Santayana, George. 1910. *Three Philosophical Poets*. Cambridge: Harvard University Press

Schoder, Raymond V. 1971–2. 'Vergil's Poetic Use of the Cumae Area.' *Classical Journal* 67: 97–109

Segal, Charles P. 1965–6. '*Aeternum per Saecula Nomen*, The Golden Bough and the Tragedy of History.' *Arion* 4: 617–57 and 5: 34–72

– 1968. 'The Hesitation of the Golden Bough: A Reexamination.' *Hermes* 96: 74–9

– 1990. 'Dido's Hesitation in *Aeneid* 4.' *Classical World* 84: 1–12

Seidel, Michael, and Edward Mendelson ed. 1977. *Homer to Brecht: The European Epic and Dramatic Traditions*. New Haven: Yale University Press

Servius. *See* Thilo and Hagen

Spencer, Stewart, and Barry Millington. 1987. *Selected Letters of Richard Wagner*. New York: W.W. Norton

Spender, Stephen. 1958. *Great Writings of Goethe*. New York: Mentor

Staines, David. Trans. 1990. *The Complete Romances of Chrétien de Troyes*. Bloomington: Indiana University Press

Stanford, W.B. 1959 (1947). *The Odyssey*. 2 vols. Basingstoke and London: Macmillan, St Martin's Press

– 1968 (1954). *The Ulysses Theme*. Ann Arbor: University of Michigan Press

Steiner, George. 1989. *Real Presences*. Chicago: University of Chicago Press

Steiner, George, and Robert Fagles, ed. 1962. *Homer: A Collection of Critical Essays*. Englewood Cliffs, NJ: Prentice-Hall

Stocker, Arthur F. 1980. 'Vergil in the Service of Augustus.' *Vergilius* 26: 1–9

Syme, Ronald. 1939. *The Roman Revolution*. Oxford: Clarendon Press

Tanner, R.G. 1970–1. 'Some Problems in *Aeneid* 7–12.' *Proceedings of the Virgil Society* 10: 37–44

Taylor, Charles H. Jr, ed. 1963. *Essays on the Odyssey*. Bloomington: Indiana University Press

Thilo, Georg, and Hermann Hagen, ed. 1961 (1884). *Servii Grammatici qui feruntur in Vergilii Carmina Commentaria*. Vol. 2. Hildesheim: Georg Olms Verlagsbuchhandlung

Thompson, Stith. 1966 (1955–8). *Motif-index of Folk-Literature*. 6 vols, rev. Bloomington: Indiana University Press

Truntz, Erich. 1963. *Goethes Faust Kommentiert*. Hamburg: Christian Wegner Verlag

Van Doren, Mark. 1950. *Don Quixote's Profession*. New York: Columbia University Press

Vann, Gerald. 1959. *The Paradise Tree*. London: Collins

– 1962. *Myth, Symbol, and Revelation*. Washington: Thomist Press

Vickery, John B., ed. 1966. *Myth and Literature*. Lincoln: University of Nebraska Press

Vickery, John B., and J'nan Sellery. 1969. *Goethe's Faust Part One: Essays in Criticism*. Belmont, Calif.: Wadsworth Publishing Company

Viëtor, Karl. 1949. *Goethe the Poet*. Trans. Moses Hadas. New York: Russell & Russell

– 1950. *Goethe the Thinker*. Trans. B.Q. Morgan. Cambridge: Harvard University Press

Vinaver, Eugène. 1980. 'The Questing Knight.' In McCune 1980, 124–40

Wagner, Richard. 1911–16. *Sämtliche Schriften und Dichtungen (Volksausgabe)*. 12 vols. Leipzig: Breitkopf and Härtel

Waite, Arthur Edward. 1933. *The Holy Grail: Its Legends and Symbolism*. London: Rider and Co.

Wayne, Philip. Trans. 1949 and 1959. *Goethe: Faust, Part One and Part Two*. Harmondsworth: Penguin Books

Weber, Clifford. 1995. 'The Allegory of the Golden Bough.' *Vergilius* 41: 3–34

West, David. 1990 (1987). 'The Bough and the Gate.' In Harrison 1990, 224–38

Weston, Jessie L. 1957 (1920). *From Ritual to Romance*. Garden City, NY: Doubleday Anchor Books

White, T.H. 1958 (1939, 1940). *The Once and Future King*. New York: G.P. Putnam's Sons

Whitman, Cedric H. 1958. *Homer and the Heroic Tradition*. Cambridge: Harvard University Press

Wilkinson, Elizabeth M., and L.A. Willoughby. 1962. *Goethe: Poet and Thinker*. London: Edward Arnold Ltd

Wilkinson, L.P. 1969. *The Georgics of Virgil*. Cambridge: Cambridge University Press

Williams, R.D. 1972. *Virgil: The Aeneid*. 2 vols. Basingstoke and London: Macmillan, St Martin's Press

Wiltshire, Susan Ford. 1989. *Public and Private in Vergil's Aeneid*. Amherst: University of Massachusetts Press

Index